human rights first

Jails and Jumpsuits

Transforming the U.S. Immigration Detention System— A Two-Year Review

October 2011

About Human Rights First

Human Rights First believes that building respect for human rights and the rule of law will help ensure the dignity to which every individual is entitled and will stem tyranny, extremism, intolerance, and violence.

Human Rights First protects people at risk: refugees who flee persecution, victims of crimes against humanity or other mass human rights violations, victims of discrimination, those whose rights are eroded in the name of national security, and human rights advocates who are targeted for defending the rights of others. These groups are often the first victims of societal instability and breakdown; their treatment is a harbinger of wider-scale repression. Human Rights First works to prevent violations against these groups and to seek justice and accountability for violations against them.

Human Rights First is practical and effective. We advocate for change at the highest levels of national and international policymaking. We seek justice through the courts. We raise awareness and understanding through the media. We build coalitions among those with divergent views. And we mobilize people to act.

Human Rights First is a non-profit, non-partisan international human rights organization based in New York and Washington D.C. To maintain our independence, we accept no government funding.

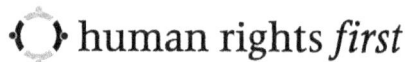

{ } human rights *first*

New York   Washington D.C.

333 Seventh Avenue	100 Maryland Avenue, NE
13th Floor	Suite 500
New York, NY 10001-5108	Washington, DC 20002-5625
Tel.: 212.845.5200	Tel: 202.547.5692
Fax: 212.845.5299	Fax: 202.543.5999

www.humanrightsfirst.org

This report is available online at www.humanrightsfirst.org.

Acknowledgements

The principal authors of this report were Ruthie Epstein and Eleanor Acer, and Ms. Epstein was the primary researcher. Additional research, writing, and editing were contributed by Annie Sovcik. Research and/or editing assistance was provided by Brett George, Abraham Paulos, Lori Adams, Elise Dunton, Sara Faust, Alyssa Rickard, Tad Stahnke, and Isabel Toolan. Sarah Graham designed the report.

We wish to thank the many refugees and asylum seekers, legal representation organizations, faith-based and community groups, corrections professionals, and officials from the Departments of Homeland Security and Justice who provided information included in this report. We also wish to express appreciation to the experts who reviewed drafts of this report, including Michele Deitch, Helen Harnett, Donald Kerwin, Steve J. Martin, and Dr. Dora Schriro, as well as to David Shapiro, who provided invaluable research guidance.

Human Rights First gratefully acknowledges the Fund for New Jersey and the Fund for New Citizens of the New York Community Trust for their generous support of our pro bono legal representation program for indigent refugees who seek asylum in the United States. We also thank the Oak Foundation for its support of the Refugee Protection Program and our work relating to the detention of asylum seekers and other immigrants.

Contents

Executive Summary

"We were real prisoners... They put us in prison even though we didn't do anything. We didn't understand anything."

–Refugee from Democratic Republic of Congo who was detained in 2011 with her younger sister in a county jail in New York alongside criminal inmates

Two years ago, the U.S. Department of Homeland Security (DHS) and Immigration and Customs Enforcement (ICE) committed to transform the U.S. immigration detention system by shifting it away from its longtime reliance on jails and jail-like facilities, to facilities with conditions more appropriate for the detention of civil immigration law detainees. At the time of these commitments, in announcements in August and October of 2009, DHS and ICE recognized that detention beds were in facilities that were "largely designed for penal, not civil, detention." In fact, many criminal correctional facilities actually offer less restrictive conditions than those typically found in immigration detention facilities, and corrections experts have confirmed that less restrictive conditions can help ensure safety in a secure facility. DHS and ICE have consistently affirmed intentions to carry out the planned reforms in a budget-neutral way.

Yet two years later, the overwhelming majority of detained asylum seekers and other civil immigration law detainees are still held in jails or jail-like facilities—almost 400,000 detainees each year, at a cost of over $2 billion. At these facilities, asylum seekers and other immigrants wear prison uniforms and are typically locked in one large room for up to 23 hours a day; they have limited or essentially no outdoor access, and visit with family only

South Texas Detention Center in Pearsall holds almost 1,500 ICE detainees.

through Plexiglas barriers, and sometimes only via video, even when visitors are in the same building.

Over the last two years, ICE has begun to use, or has acknowledged plans to use, five new facilities that would contain in total 3,485 detention beds in less penal conditions. These conditions would include increased outdoor access, contact visitation with families, and "non-institutional" (though still uniform) clothing for some detainees. These facilities are designed as templates for a more appropriate approach to immigration detention. If they open as designed and as scheduled, 14 percent of ICE's detained asylum seeker and immigrant population would be housed in these less-penal conditions— meaning that 86 percent of ICE detainees would still be held in jails and jail-like facilities. Official standards detailing core requirements for the environment and conditions of a civil detention system—covering matters such as dress, movement within facilities, extended outdoor access, and contact visitation with family—have not been developed or implemented.

ICE has also taken important steps to improve other aspects of the immigration detention system—such as creating a system to allow families and counsel to learn the name of the facility where an immigration detainee is held, issuing new guidance on parole assessments for detained arriving asylum seekers, and training new ICE monitors to report back to headquarters on compliance with standards in the field. However, this report focuses primarily on the agency's progress on its commitment to "literally overhaul the system"—to transition the immigration detention system away from its jail-oriented approach to a system with conditions more appropriate for civil immigration detainees. While ICE did indicate that the shift would take place "in three to five years," two years in, there is still a long way to go.

Jails and jail-like facilities have been found to be inappropriate and unnecessarily costly for asylum seekers and other civil immigration detainees by the U.S. government itself, as well as by bipartisan groups and international human rights bodies. In a major 2005 study requested by Congress, the bipartisan U.S. Commission on International Religious Freedom (USCIRF) and its expert on prison systems observed that most of the facilities used by DHS to detain asylum seekers and other immigrants "in most critical respects...are structured and operated much like standardized correctional facilities," resembling "in every essential respect, conventional jails." The Council on Foreign Relations bipartisan task force on immigration policy, co-chaired by Jeb Bush and Thomas McLarty, concurred in July 2009 that "[i]n many cases asylum seekers are forced to wear prison uniforms [and] held in jails and jail-like facilities." The bipartisan Constitution Project's Liberty and Security Committee similarly concluded in December 2009 that "[d]espite the nominally 'civil'—as opposed to 'criminal'—nature of their alleged offenses, non-citizens are often held in state and local jails." In 2009, DHS's own Special Advisor—who has run two state prison systems and currently serves as Commissioner of Correction in New York City—concluded in a report prepared for DHS and ICE that:

> With only a few exceptions, the facilities that ICE uses to detain aliens were built, and operate, as jails and prisons to confine pre-trial and

sentenced felons. ICE relies primarily on correctional incarceration standards designed for pre-trial felons and on correctional principles of care, custody, and control. These standards impose more restrictions and carry more costs than are necessary to effectively manage the majority of the detained population.

The use of immigration detention facilities that are penal in nature is inconsistent with U.S. commitments under the 1951 Convention Relating to the Status of Refugees and its Protocol, as well as the International Covenant on Civil and Political Rights. The Inter-American Commission on Human Rights and the U.N. Special Rapporteur on the Human Rights of Migrants have both expressed concern, in reports issued in 2010 and 2008, respectively, about the punitive and jail-like conditions used by the U.S. government in its immigration detention system. Even with more appropriate detention conditions, however, detention can still be—and is—penal in nature when the detention itself runs afoul of other human rights protections—for example, when detention is not necessary, reasonable, or proportionate, or is unnecessarily prolonged.

In an April 2009 report, Human Rights First documented the significant increase in the use of jail-like facilities to detain asylum seekers and other immigration detainees in the United States. In that report, Human Rights First found that the U.S. immigration detention system lacks basic due process safeguards to prevent unnecessary or prolonged detention of asylum seekers, and that DHS's use of jail and jail-like facilities had actually increased—rather than decreased—since USCIRF's 2005 recommendation that DHS and ICE phase out their reliance on these facilities.

In this report, Human Rights First focuses its review on the progress of DHS and ICE in transforming the U.S. immigration detention system away from its reliance on jails and jail-like facilities to a system with conditions more appropriate for civil immigration law detainees. In the course of our assessment, we visited 17 ICE-authorized detention facilities that together held more than 10,000 of the 33,400 total ICE beds; interviewed government officials, legal service providers, and former immigration detainees; and reviewed existing government data on the U.S. immigration detention system. We also interviewed a range of former prison wardens, corrections officials, and other experts on correctional systems.

Human Rights First's Primary Findings

■ **Asylum Seekers and Other Immigrants Are Still Overwhelmingly Held in Jails and Jail-like Facilities**. In July 2009, approximately 50 percent of ICE's population was held in actual correctional facilities that also housed criminal detainees. Since DHS announced its intention to reform the detention system, there has been no decrease in that proportion. The remaining 50 percent of ICE immigration detainees—those who are not held in actual jails or prisons—are still held in jail-like facilities. These facilities are surrounded by multiple perimeter fences usually topped with razor wire, barbed wire, or concertina coils. Detainees typically wear color-coded prison uniforms and live in conditions that are characteristic of penal facilities— their freedom of movement and outdoor access are highly limited; they often visit with friends and loved ones separated by Plexiglas barriers; and they have little or no privacy in toilets and showers. Since 2009, ICE has added or made plans to add more than 2,700 new jail and jail-like beds to the system. ICE reports that these beds will reduce transfers by realigning the agency's bed "needs" with bed "capacity," and at the same time will keep detainees closer to family members, community resources, and legal counsel.

■ **Immigration Detention Costs U.S. Taxpayers Over $2 Billion Each Year.** The U.S. government will spend more than $2 billion for immigration detention next year. The costs of immigration detention have risen dramatically over the past 15 years, as detention capacity has more than tripled— from 108,454 detainees in 1996 to approximately 363,000 in 2010. Congress has consistently appropriated the funds to sustain and expand the immigration detention system—from $864 million seven years ago to $2.02 billion today, an increase of 134 percent. ICE projects that for fiscal year 2012 it will pay an average of $122 per day per detainee. ICE has not expanded Alternatives to Detention nationwide – which can save $110 per day per detainee - and its requested fiscal year 2012 budget for detention is 28 times its requested budget for Alternatives to Detention.

■ **ICE Continues to Rely on Detention Standards Modeled on Correctional Standards.** Despite the commitment by both DHS and ICE to develop new standards to reflect the environment and conditions appropriate for civil immigration detention, immigration detention facilities are still inspected— just as they were in 2009 when ICE announced its reform plans—under standards that are modeled on those used in prisons and jails, and that impose more restrictions and costs than are necessary to effectively manage the majority of the immigration detention population, as detailed by both the 2009 DHS-ICE report and the 2005 USCIRF report. Though ICE has revised these existing corrections-based standards, the revised standards, which have not yet been implemented in any facility, do not call for the types of conditions—including in areas relating to dress, extended outdoor access, contact visitation, and improved privacy—that would reflect the new environment and conditions for civil immigration detention

■ **ICE Has Taken Some Steps Toward Less Penal Detention Conditions, But Only a Small Portion of Detainees Will See Change.** Since the reform announcements, ICE has developed plans for several facilities that are anticipated to offer conditions less penal than those in the majority of existing ICE facilities. The conditions at these facilities—in Texas, Florida, Illinois, California, and New Jersey—are anticipated to provide for some increased outdoor access, greater mobility between areas within the closed facility and its grounds, contact visitation with families, and "non-institutional" clothing (though outdoor access will still be limited, and detainees will not be permitted to wear their own clothing). If these facilities open as designed and scheduled, ICE would potentially have 3,485 new beds with less penal conditions. ICE's existing less-penal beds—in Texas, Florida, and Pennsylvania—number 1,137. Altogether, these 4,622 new beds would comprise 14 percent of ICE's detained asylum seeker and immigrant population— meaning that 86 percent of ICE detainees would still be held in jails and jail-like facilities.

■ **Less-Restrictive Conditions Can Help Ensure Safety in Both Corrections Facilities and Immigration Detention Facilities.** Though ICE and DHS have called these conditions "non-penal," many of the conditions proposed actually exist in the corrections context as well—or should exist in any facility that detains or incarcerates—and are touted as best practices to improve facility safety and humane treatment for many prison populations. Human Rights First interviewed former prison wardens, corrections experts, and long-time corrections officials who confirmed that a normalized environment—one that replicates as much as possible life on the outside—helps to ensure the safety and security of any detention facility. Multiple studies examining the impact of prison design and operations on safety draw the same conclusion.

- **ICE Has Not Expanded Cost-Effective Alternatives to Detention Nationwide, and Asylum Seekers and Other Immigration Detainees Continue to Be Detained Unnecessarily—and at Substantial Cost—Due to Lack of Effective Release Procedures**. Alternatives to Detention (ATD) programs generally provide for release from immigration detention with some additional measures to monitor the individual after release. Several different community-based ATD programs have been successfully tested in the United States, leading to substantial cost-savings and high compliance rates. In its October 2009 reform announcements, ICE highlighted the cost-effectiveness of "alternatives to detention." In April 2010, it submitted a report to Congress describing several scenarios for nationwide expansion of ATDs, which states that ATDs costs ICE on average $8.88 per day per individual – more than $110 a day less than detention. Meanwhile, ICE's requested budget for detention in fiscal year 2012 was $2.02 billion—28 times its requested budget for Alternatives to Detention. At the same time, U.S. laws and regulations governing the detention and release of asylum seekers and other immigration detainees remain inconsistent with U.S. commitments under the Refugee Convention, its Protocol, and other human rights standards. During 2010, DHS and DOJ declined to take steps to provide access to immigration court custody hearings for asylum seekers who are detained after requesting protection at U.S. airports and borders.

- **Detained Asylum Seekers and Other Immigrants Do Not Have Adequate Access to Legal Assistance and Fair Procedures, Particularly in Isolated Detention Facilities**. The overwhelming majority of detained asylum seekers and other immigrants—84 percent—are not represented by legal counsel in removal proceedings, the legal process through which ICE seeks their deportation. In fact, most do not even receive basic information about immigration law and process through the highly successful Legal Orientation Program (LOP) managed by the DOJ's Executive Office for Immigration Review (EOIR). Despite the extraordinary need for legal information in this context, bipartisan support for LOP, the efficiencies enhanced by providing respondents with basic information, and the President's fiscal year 2012 budget request to expand the program, Congress has funded EOIR to operate the LOP in just 25 detention facilities, reaching approximately 15 percent of detained immigrants and 35 percent of detained immigrants in EOIR proceedings annually. The isolating nature of detention, as well as the rural location of many facilities, makes accessing legal counsel, especially pro bono or low cost legal counsel, extraordinarily difficult. The remote locations also mean that removal hearings for detained asylum seekers and other immigrants are often conducted via video-conference rather than in person. According to Human Rights First calculations, almost 40 percent of ICE's total bed space is located more than 60 miles from an urban center.

- **ICE Has Taken Steps to Improve Other Aspects of the Existing System, Though Additional Steps Are Necessary.** This report focuses primarily on ICE's commitments to shift away from reliance on jails and jail-like facilities. At the same time, however, ICE has taken some meaningful steps forward in other areas of detention reform. The agency has centralized management of all contracts in a single office and reduced the number of facilities from 341 to 254. It launched an online detainee locator that allows family and legal counsel to find out where an individual is being held. It developed a risk classification assessment tool for its officers to use in order to systematize detainee release and/or custody classification decisions and improve oversight of these decisions, addressing a major management gap in the detention system. It revised the parole policy so that all detained arriving asylum seekers in expedited removal who pass credible fear screening interviews are required to be assessed for potential parole eligibility. ICE has developed a detainee transfer policy that, when implemented, is intended to systematize transfer practices, and has trained and placed in the field 42 facility monitors who report back to Washington on standards compliance. In June 2011, the agency issued new guidance on the use of prosecutorial discretion by ICE personnel, which may impact detention and release decisions, and in August 2011, the Administration announced plans to review 300,000 cases in removal proceedings, including detained cases, and administratively close the cases of low-priority individuals, which has the potential to reduce the backlog of cases in immigration courts and improve case processing times. These are all welcome improvements to policy and practice that should exist for any system that detains or incarcerates people, whether correctional or civil in nature.

Moving Forward: Key Conditions in a "Civil" Immigration Detention System

"Civil detention"—in this case, detention that is appropriate to ICE's civil detention authority—is legally distinct from criminal detention, but few examples exist to demonstrate what civil detention actually looks like in terms of conditions and environment. ICE has developed a Statement of Objectives to describe its vision to potential contractors and local governments that may construct or operate new "civil" facilities (though ICE offers no analogous guide to reform for administrators of existing facilities). These facilities would be secure facilities—that is, they would be surrounded by a secure perimeter to prevent detainees from leaving—and would permit detainees to move somewhat more freely within the facility, including to outdoor recreation. Detainees would have access to contact visits and some privacy in showers and toilets, and they would wear "non-institutional" clothing.

One existing ICE facility, Berks Family Residential Center in Pennsylvania, provides a model that could be replicated. It allows detainees to move freely within certain areas of the facility, it permits contact visits and extended outdoor access, detainees enjoy privacy in toilets and showers, and detainees can wear their own clothing. ICE could create these conditions within a facility surrounded by a secure perimeter for the majority of its detainee population. Two other existing ICE facilities, Broward Transitional Center in Florida and Hutto Detention Center in Texas, also provide some less penal conditions, including expanded freedom of movement and outdoor access and contact visits; at Hutto, detainees can also wear their own clothing.

Human Rights First urges ICE—over the next two years—to prioritize its commitment to move the U.S. immigration detention system away from its reliance on jails and jail-like facilities. Instead, all facilities holding ICE detainees should include a range of conditions, programming, and other measures more appropriate for immigration law detainees. Some of the conditions that should exist in all immigration detention facilities—and that should be detailed in new standards that govern them—include:

- **Increased freedom of movement within a secure facility.** Using a proven custody classification tool appropriate to the ICE civil detainee population, as well as modern technology, ICE should provide immigration detainees with the ability to move freely within a closed facility and its grounds, among their housing unit, outdoor recreation area, indoor recreation or common space, library, cafeteria, and any other program or support area throughout the day. Rather than multiple daily counts, which disrupt the day by requiring detainees to remain in their housing units for up to an hour at a time, ICE could use a check-in system modeled on the system already in use at Hutto Detention Center.

- **Non-prison clothing for detainees.** Individuals who are detained for administrative purposes under the immigration law should be allowed to wear their own clothing, or, at the very least, clothing that does not resemble uniforms. Two immigration detention facilities—the Hutto Detention Center and the Berks Family Residential Center—operate without prison uniforms already, and ICE's family residential standards permit detainees to wear their own clothing and require that the facility provide to those who need it clothing that "shall not resemble institutional style clothing." Both the Inter-American Commission on Human Rights and the UN Special Rapporteur on the Human Rights of Migrants have specifically identified the use of prison uniforms as one of the factors that make U.S. immigration detention punitive.

■ **Contact visits.** All ICE-authorized facilities should permit contact visits for all ICE detainees. The prison systems in all 50 states permit contact visits for inmates in their custody. Contact visits are also permitted in all federal Bureau of Prisons facilities, which hold in total more than 200,000 federal inmates. ICE should ensure that the visitation schedule allows visitors, especially those traveling a distance, ample time to spend with their detained family members or friends, during both weekends and weekdays, and that visitors are not forced to wait extended periods of time due to lack of adequate visitation space. Video visitation should not be used as a substitute for in-person visits.

■ **Privacy in showers and toilets.** All ICE facilities should provide some degree of privacy in showers and toilets for all ICE detainees. Open-bay or "gang" showers and toilets should not be used for civil immigration law detainees.

■ **True outdoor recreation with expanded access.** All ICE facilities should have outdoor recreation areas that are actually outside, accessible to detainees throughout the day, with dedicated space for sports and other physical activities, as well as grassy and shaded areas to allow for outdoor access during very hot or inclement weather. Fresh air and natural light should not be blocked. Corrections experts and ICE facility administrators acknowledge the importance of outdoor recreation to occupy detainees and help ensure facility safety.

■ **Programming and activities.** ICE should ensure all detainees have access to daily programming and activities, including access to email, which is a standard form of communication and is now available throughout the federal prison system.

Some ICE officers and managers have questioned whether ICE's promised shift away from a prison model of detention for civil immigration law detainees would undermine the safety of officers and detainees. While the new facilities designed by ICE are intended to offer fewer unnecessary restrictions than more jail-oriented facilities, the conditions in these new facilities would be similar to those in low- and minimum-security federal prisons, but with the addition of a secure perimeter. As detailed in this report, multiple studies, as well as former corrections officials and other experts, have concluded that a normalized detention environment can help improve

safety and security at facilities holding higher-risk detainees as well as low-risk detainees. One corrections expert who spent his career in the Texas prison system told Human Rights First: "The extent that you can normalize the confinement setting is the extent to which you can have a safe environment." Individuals who present a particular risk to officers and other facility staff or to other detainees should be identified—and appropriately placed separate from lower-risk detainees—using an effective risk classification assessment tool. ICE should require that less penal and more normalized conditions exist for the vast majority of asylum seekers and other immigration detainees held in secure detention facilities—not just a small percentage.

Recommendations

Thorough reform of the U.S. detention system will require a combination of legislative, regulatory, and administrative actions. At the end of this report, we have detailed a series of recommendations that will improve U.S. detention policies and practices in general and for the victims of persecution who seek this country's protection. These recommended reforms include:

1. **Stop Using Prisons, Jails, and Jail-like Facilities, and When Detention Is Necessary Use Facilities with Conditions Appropriate for Civil Immigration Law Detainees.** Over the next two years, DHS and ICE should move forward on their commitments to transform the current detention system modeled on jails and prisons to one with conditions appropriate for civil immigration law detainees, including:

   ☐ **End the Use of Jails and Prisons.** Immigration and Customs Enforcement should phase out contracts with county and state jails and prisons, which are inappropriate for civil immigration law detainees. ICE should also end the use of jail-like detention facilities.

   ☐ **Use More Appropriate Facilities.** After an individualized assessment of whether detention is necessary, when asylum seekers and other immigrants are detained under the civil immigration laws, they should not be held in prisons, jails, or jail-like facilities. Instead, **Immigration and Customs Enforcement** should use facilities with more appropriate conditions that provide a more normalized environment, permitting detainees to wear their own clothing, move freely among various areas within a secure facility and grounds, access true outdoor recreation for extended periods of time, access programming and email, have some privacy in toilets and showers, and have contact visits with family and friends. As detailed in this report, normalized living conditions in detention can actually help improve safety inside a facility.

☐ **Develop and Implement New Standards Specifying Conditions for Civil Immigration Detention**. Within one year, **Immigration and Customs Enforcement** should develop new residential detention standards that require all facilities to include the key elements outlined in this report—including permitting detainees to wear their own clothing, move freely among various areas within a secure facility and grounds, access true outdoor recreation for extended periods of time, access programming and email, have some privacy in toilets and showers, and have contact visits with family and friends. To promote compliance, these new standards should be incorporated into contracts and promulgated into regulations.

☐ **Reform Existing Immigration Detention Facilities.** While existing jail-like facilities remain inappropriate for civil immigration law detainees, some reforms can be implemented at these facilities while the transition to facilities with more appropriate conditions moves forward. In these existing facilities, **Immigration and Customs Enforcement** should ensure that non-prison clothing, contact visits, true and expanded outdoor recreation, and privacy for showers and toilets are instituted within six months. The changes made since 2007 at Hutto Detention Center in Texas can serve as a model for reforms to existing facilities.

☐ **Use Automated and Effective Risk Classification Assessment Tool to Identify and Properly Place Any Detainees Who Present Safety Risks in Custody**. **Immigration and Customs Enforcement** should complete the process of automating a risk classification assessment tool for use in all ICE-authorized

facilities. In addition to identifying individuals who should be released, an effective and standardized assessment tool can identify individuals who may pose a risk to officers or to other detainees, and in such cases, ICE can ensure appropriate placement separate from lower-risk detainees, or other measures proportionate to the risk, to improve safety. In taking such measures, ICE should not automatically hold in a correctional setting all detainees with criminal convictions. Further, a risk assessment tool is a management tool— not a substitute for independent review of the need to detain.

2. **Prevent Unnecessary Costs by Ensuring that Asylum Seekers and Other Immigrants Are Not Detained Unnecessarily.** The creation of facilities with more appropriate conditions should not be used as a reason to detain individuals who present no risks and meet the requirements for release, including through an alternative to detention where additional supervision is necessary to ensure compliance.

☐ **Expand Alternatives to Detention Nationwide. Immigration and Customs Enforcement** should create an effective nationwide system of ATDs for those who cannot be released without additional supervision, utilizing full-service community-based models that provide individualized case management, increasing access to legal and social service providers through meaningful referrals, as well as access to information about court and case information. When used as true alternatives to detention for individuals who would not otherwise be released—and not as alternatives to release for the non-detained population in removal proceedings—ATD programs should create significant cost savings for the government—more than $110 per person per day. **Congress** should ensure that cost savings are realized in the expansion of this program by reallocating part of the detention and removal budget to an increase in the ATD budget.

☐ **Provide Immigration Court Custody Hearings for All Detainees.** The **Departments of Justice** and Homeland Security should revise regulatory language and/or **Congress** should enact legislation to provide arriving asylum seekers and other immigration detainees with the chance to have their custody reviewed in a hearing before an immigration court.

☐ **Revise Laws to Provide for Detention** *Only* **After Individualized Assessment of Need to Detain. Congress** should revise laws so that an asylum seeker or other immigrant may be detained only after an assessment of the need for detention in his or her individual case, rather than through automatic or mandatory detention.

3. **Improve Access to Legal Assistance and Fair Procedures**. The **Department of Justice, Department of Homeland Security** and **Immigration and Customs Enforcement** should work with **Congress** to ensure that detained asylum seekers and other immigration detainees have sufficient access to legal representation, legal information, and in-person hearings of their asylum claims and deportation cases, including by ending the use of facilities in remote locations that undermine access to legal representation, medical care, and family; ensuring that Legal Orientation Presentations are funded and in place at all facilities detaining asylum seekers and other immigration detainees; and ensuring that in-person Immigration Judges and Asylum Officers are available for all detained asylum seekers or other immigration detainees.

4. **Take Other Steps to Address Deficiencies in Immigration Detention Conditions.** Though the agency has taken some steps toward improving conditions in the existing system, serious deficiencies persist. **Immigration and Customs Enforcement** should implement a number of improvements in all facilities housing immigration detainees, including by taking additional steps to ensure high-quality medical and mental health treatment, adopting the standards recommended by the bipartisan federal National Prison Rape Elimination Commission, improving training for officers and staff (whether employed by ICE, local government, or a private contractor) with the support of the **DHS Office of Civil rights and Civil Liberties**, and improving communication between headquarters and the field.

Introduction

"What is our detention power? Our detention power is civil in nature. We're not a penal institution. We detain people for purposes of removal. We detain people because if we release them they would pose a danger to people or run away. We're not incarcerating anyone."

> –ICE Assistant Secretary John Morton, 2010[1]

"The paradigm was wrong."

> –DHS Secretary Janet Napolitano, 2009[2]

"Even the detention by DRO [Detention and Removal Operations—ICE's detention division] of those with criminal convictions is strictly administrative in nature, not punitive. This necessitates different environments, standards, and population management within DRO facilities than that of other federal, state, county, or local correctional facilities."

> –DHS/ICE ten-year strategic plan, 2003[3]

Each year, the U.S. government detains close to 400,000 asylum seekers and other immigration law detainees in more than 250 jails and jail-like facilities nationwide. In these facilities, immigration detainees typically wear color-coded prison uniforms and live in conditions that are characteristic of penal facilities—their freedom of movement and outdoor access are highly limited; they often visit with family and friends separated by Plexiglas barriers; and they have little or no privacy in toilets and showers. They are subject to multiple daily head counts, and they often have limited access to programming and must eat their meals in their housing units.

Immigration detention has more than tripled over the past 15 years. In 1996, the Immigration and Naturalization Service (INS) detained 108,454 immigrants. In 2003, Immigration and Customs Enforcement (ICE)—the interior immigration enforcement agency within the Department of Homeland Security, which took over immigration functions from the INS that year—detained 223,898 immigrants. By 2010, that number had increased to approximately 363,000.[4]

IMMIGRATION DETENTION AND U.S. INTERNATIONAL HUMAN RIGHTS OBLIGATIONS

In the wake of World War II, the United States played a leading role in building an international refugee protection regime to ensure that the world's nations would never again refuse to extend shelter to refugees fleeing persecution and harm. The United States has committed to the central guarantees of the 1951 Refugee Convention and its 1967 Protocol. The United States is also a party to the International Covenant on Civil and Political Rights. The guidelines of the U.N. High Commissioner for Refugees and a range of other international authorities have made clear that detention should only be used in limited circumstances; that when asylum seekers and migrants are held for purposes of administrative detention under immigration laws, they should be detained in facilities that are specially designed for these populations; and that the conditions of their detention should not be punitive or amount to a penalty.[5]

As the detained population increased during this time period, U.S. immigration authorities, rather than designing and utilizing facilities with conditions that are appropriate for civil immigration law detainees, have simply utilized available bed space in criminal prisons and jails, along with new facilities that were modeled on prisons and jails.[6] Asylum seekers and other immigration detainees are now held all over the country in a patchwork system of ICE-run facilities, facilities operated by private prison contractors, and local jails and state prisons that also hold criminal inmates. Congress has consistently appropriated the funds necessary to sustain and expand the immigration detention system—from $864 million just seven years ago, to $2.02 billion today.

The Department of Homeland Security (DHS) holds asylum seekers and other immigration detainees pursuant to its authority under civil immigration laws. These detainees are not being held as punishment for crimes, and their detention is considered civil or administrative in nature. The purpose of immigration detention, according to DHS and ICE, is limited: to ensure that detainees show up for their deportation hearings, and that they comply with deportation orders if necessary.[7]

In a major 2005 study authorized by Congress, the bipartisan U.S. Commission on International Religious Freedom (USCIRF) found that most of the facilities used by DHS and ICE to detain asylum seekers and other immigrants "in most critical respects... are structured and operated much like standardized correctional facilities," resembling, "in every essential respect, conventional jails."[8] The Commission found that these facilities were inappropriate for asylum seekers (who were the subject of the Commission's study) and recommended that when they are detained, they instead be held in "non-jail-like" facilities.[9]

In an April 2009 report, Human Rights First found that instead of decreasing reliance on jails and jail-like detention following USCIRF's recommendations, DHS and ICE had instead increased their use of these facilities—adding an additional 9,000 beds in jails and jail-like facilities since the Commission had issued its report in February 2005.[10] Human Rights First recommended that DHS and ICE stop using jails and jail-like facilities to detain asylum seekers and other immigration detainees, and that detention standards be

WHO'S IN DETENTION?

Each day, ICE holds in detention up to 33,400 non-citizens it is seeking to deport, for a total of almost 400,000 per year. These immigration detainees include asylum seekers fleeing persecution in their home country, legal immigrants who overstayed their visas, recent border crossers, and lawful permanent residents who were charged with or convicted of non-violent or violent crimes that subject them to mandatory detention or that may make them removable.

The numbers below demonstrate that a large proportion of ICE detainees have been classified by the agency itself as low risk or non-criminal, and only a small percentage have been convicted of violent crimes. Over the past two years, the breakdown has not shifted, according to ICE's own data.

On July 18, 2011, the ICE detainee population totaled 31,065. Of those:

■ 3,855 Level 1 detainees (lowest risk) were held in actual jails.

■ 4,645 non-criminal detainees were held in actual jails.[11]

On May 2, 2011, the ICE detainee population totaled 32,596. Of those:

■ 13,311—41 percent—were classified as Level 1 detainees (lowest risk)

■ 6,050—19 percent—were classified as Level 3 detainees (highest risk)[12]

■ 14,522—45 percent—were non-criminals

On September 1, 2009, the ICE detainee population totaled 31,075. Of those:

■ 11 percent had committed violent crimes

■ The majority were low-custody.[13]

In October 2011, ICE advised Human Rights First that: "Fully 90 percent of the Average Daily Population at ICE detention facilities during FY11 were detained either because their detention was mandatory by law or because their cases fell into one of the agency's three immigration enforcement priorities. The remaining 10 percent includes detainees who were arrested for serious criminal violations for which they haven't yet been convicted, and individuals who spent as little as one night in a holding cell before being released."[14]

revised to provide for detention in which individuals can wear their own clothing (rather than prison uniforms); have contact visitation (as opposed to visits through Plexiglas barriers) with family and friends; and have freedom of movement within secure facilities (so they can use outdoor areas, libraries, indoor recreation or cafeteria areas during the course of the day).

In January 2009, USCIRF expressed its concern that, "contrary to USCIRF recommendations, DHS's use of jails and jail-like facilities has increased in the past few years."[15] The Council on Foreign Relations bipartisan task force on immigration policy, co-chaired by Jeb Bush and Thomas McLarty, observed in July 2009 that "[i]n many cases asylum seekers are forced to wear prison uniforms [and] held in jails and jail-like facilities."[16] The bipartisan Constitution Project's Liberty and Security Committee similarly concluded in December 2009 that "[d]espite the nominally 'civil'—as opposed to 'criminal'—nature of their alleged offenses, non-citizens are often held in state and local jails; others among them may be held in sub-standard, remote facilities."[17] Many other reports—from the media, nongovernmental organizations, and U.S. government agencies—documented a range of problems with the U.S. immigration detention system, including significant deficiencies in medical care.[18]

As detailed in the next section, in August and October 2009 DHS and ICE announced plans for a wide-ranging overhaul of the immigration detention system. ICE Assistant Secretary John Morton stated: "With these reforms, ICE will move away from our present, decentralized, jail-oriented approach to a system wholly designed for and based on ICE's civil detention authorities."[19]

In this report, Human Rights First assesses the government's progress in meeting its commitments and advancing a true shift away from a jail model for immigration detention, to a model that reflects conditions that are more appropriate for civil immigration law

detainees. While the report also briefly outlines some of the other reforms advanced by U.S. authorities to the existing immigration detention system and some continuing deficiencies in release procedures, in order to provide a broader picture of ongoing detention reforms and challenges, this report is focused primarily on the shift from a jail-oriented approach to immigration detention toward an approach that utilizes conditions and environments more appropriate for civil immigration detainees. In 2010 and 2011, Human Rights First researchers visited 17 ICE-authorized detention facilities that together held more than 10,000 of the 33,400 total ICE beds.[20] These facilities included ICE-operated Service Processing Centers, privately operated Contract Detention Facilities, and county jails and prisons operating under Intergovernmental Service Agreements with ICE. The majority of the detainees at these facilities had no criminal history or only a nonviolent criminal history (many of which are immigration-related crimes, such as illegal border crossing).[21] In total, at the time of our visits, the 17 facilities detained hundreds of asylum seekers, as well as thousands of other immigration detainees in removal proceedings.

We interviewed federal government officials, local government officials, legal service providers, and former immigration detainees. We also interviewed corrections officials, former corrections officials, and experts and consultants who deal with prison systems. In addition, we reviewed existing government and nongovernmental organization reports, other data on the U.S. immigration detention system, publicly available Statements of Objectives, proposals, service agreements, and contracts for new or proposed immigration detention facilities.

The Shift to Civil Detention—
U.S. Government Commitments

"I intend to change the jail-oriented approach of our current detention system, and am in the process of redesigning the system so it meets our needs as an agency that detains people for civil, not penal, purposes."

–ICE Assistant Secretary John Morton, March 2010 [22]

In February 2009, DHS Secretary Janet Napolitano appointed a longtime expert on prison systems to serve as her Special Advisor on Immigration and Customs Enforcement and Detention and Removal—following years of criticism of the U.S. immigration detention system, including in a number of U.S. government reports.[23] Dr. Dora Schriro had previously run the corrections systems in Arizona and Missouri, and she currently serves as Commissioner of Correction for New York City. The new DHS Special Advisor spent the next six months visiting detention facilities across the country, analyzing DHS and ICE data and other records, and reviewing reports from the federal government, the U.N. refugee agency, the American Bar Association, and many nongovernmental organizations. She also interviewed facility staff, detainees, federal, state, and local government officials, and members of Congress and their staffs. This research would result in a report that was delivered to Secretary Napolitano in September 2009 and released to the public in October 2009.[24]

Against this backdrop, DHS and ICE announced a comprehensive set of reforms to the U.S. immigration detention system. On August 6, 2009, ICE acknowledged:

> The present immigration detention system is sprawling and needs more direct federal oversight and management. While ICE has over 32,000 detention beds at any given time, the beds are spread out over as many as 350 different facilities largely designed for penal, not civil, detention. ICE employees do not run most of these. The facilities are either jails operated by county authorities or detention centers operated by private contractors.

That same day, ICE Assistant Secretary Morton outlined a round of major reforms and said, "With these reforms, ICE will move away from our present, decentralized, jail-oriented approach to a system wholly designed for and based on ICE's civil detention authorities... These same reforms will bring improved medical care, custodial conditions, fiscal prudence, and ICE oversight." The specific commitments outlined by ICE and its Assistant Secretary with respect to this transformation from a "jail-oriented approach" to a system designed for detention under "civil" authority included:[25]

■ **Facilities Designed for Immigration Detention Purposes**: The Assistant Secretary announced that "...within the next three to five years, we will detain the people within our custody in facilities designed, located, and operated specifically for immigration purposes... If we do this right, we will see that our facilities move to a much more sophisticated design and location where we have a certain level of restrictive settings and circumstances for people who pose a danger to others and to themselves, and less restrictive settings for those people who are simply a risk of flight and need to be detained, but are not otherwise a danger to people."

■ **End ICE's Primary Reliance on Penal Facilities**: An ICE fact sheet, dated August 6, stated: "The system will no longer rely primarily on excess capacity in penal institutions."[26]

■ **New Detention Standards for New Environment**:
The Assistant Secretary announced that ICE was
"going to move to new standards that reflect the new
environment and the new programs and practices."

■ **New ICE Office to Plan Civil Detention System**: The
ICE fact sheet said that ICE would "[c]reate a new
Office of Detention Policy and Planning (ODPP) to
plan and design a civil detention system tailored to
ICE's needs."

Exactly two months later, and shortly after DHS's Special
Advisor had delivered her report to DHS, on October 6,
2009, Secretary Napolitano and Assistant Secretary
Morton announced another round of detention reforms to
"address the seven major components of the detention
system" identified in the DHS Special Advisor's report.
Secretary Napolitano noted that "there is a big difference
between managing a detention system for ICE versus
running a state-prison system... This is a system that
encompasses many different types of detainees, not all
of whom need to be held in prison-like circumstances or
jail-like circumstances, which not only may be
unnecessary but more expensive than necessary."
Assistant Secretary Morton affirmed that the
recommendations of the DHS Special Advisor's report
"will form the basis of our ongoing reform efforts here at
ICE, along with the advice from our employees, detention
specialists, and immigration organizations." DHS and ICE
detailed a number of specific commitments relating to a
shift to less penal conditions:[27]

■ **New Facilities Reflecting Reform Principles**: The
DHS fact sheet, dated October 6, committed ICE to
issue two competitive bids for new facilities
reflecting core principles of detention reform,
including the principle that "ICE will detain aliens in
settings commensurate with the risk of flight and
danger they present," by the end of FY 2010.

■ **Standards to Reflect Conditions Appropriate for
Immigrant Detention Populations**: The DHS fact
sheet promised that ICE would "[r]evise immigration
detention standards to reflect the conditions
appropriate for various immigration detainee
populations" by the end of FY 2010.[28]

■ **Residential Facilities for Non-violent, Non-
criminal Detainees**: Secretary Napolitano
announced, "We will begin to house non-violent,
non-criminals such as newly arrived asylum seekers

at facilities commensurate with the risks that they
present and we will also begin efforts to house these
populations near immigration service providers and
pursue different options like converted hotels or
residential facilities for their detention."

These steps were, as Assistant Secretary Morton noted,
based in part on the October 2009 DHS-ICE report
prepared by the DHS Special Advisor. That report had
found:

> With only a few exceptions, the facilities that ICE
> uses to detain aliens were built, and operate, as
> jails and prisons to confine pre-trial and
> sentenced felons. ICE relies primarily on
> correctional incarceration standards designed for
> pre-trial felons and on correctional principles of
> care, custody, and control. These standards
> impose more restrictions and carry more costs
> than are necessary to effectively manage the
> majority of the detained population.[29]

In that report, and in subsequent Congressional
testimony, Dr. Schriro outlined a number of concrete
recommendations for reforming the U.S. immigration
detention system. These recommendations included:

■ **New Civil Detention Standards**: In her
Congressional testimony, Dr. Schriro recommended
that ICE "[d]evelop and adopt civil detention
standards and operating procedures consistent with
civil detention," focusing on "movement, meal
service, housing, dress, visitation," and other
areas.[30]

■ **Expanded Access to Outdoor Recreation and
Other Areas of Facility**: The report concluded that
movement in immigration detention facilities is
"largely restricted and detainees spend the majority
of their time in their housing units." It recommended
instead that detainees be provided with "access to
the housing unit dayroom, outdoor recreation, and
to programs and support space in other parts of the
detention facility consistent with their custody
classification..." and that "[recreation] access
should be expanded to the greatest number of hours
daily."[31]

■ **Only Use Facilities with Conditions Appropriate
for Civil Detainees:** In her Congressional testimony,
Dr. Schriro recommended that ICE use only those
facilities "whose design supports the delivery of

care, custody and control for civilly detained general and special populations." The report urged ICE to "consider, in consultation with its stakeholders, normalizing the living environment for low-custody aliens."[32]

In the 2009 announcements, DHS and ICE appear to contemplate different degrees of restrictions for various immigration detention populations. The announcements indicate a plan to house "non-violent, non-criminals" in more residential facilities, and subsequent plans have suggested that—at least at one facility—immigration detainees with "very minor, non-violent criminal records" will be held in a more normalized environment. At the same time, DHS and ICE appear to plan a higher level of restrictions—similar to the current penal model—for most detainees with criminal records. As detailed in this report, many prison systems in the United States offer less restrictive conditions than currently exist in most immigration detention facilities, and corrections professionals assert that such normalized conditions actually strengthen the safety of their facilities.

Asylum Seekers and Other Immigration Detainees Still Overwhelmingly Held in Jails and Jail-Like Facilities

"[We need to] literally overhaul the system and we need to make sure that the system we own—and operate at vast expense to the taxpayer—reflects our basic powers as an agency—that is civil detention.... I mean a much, much smaller network of dedicated ICE detention facilities designed specifically for immigration detention purposes. Facilities with plenty of telephones, open spaces, and good conditions. Facilities no more restrictive than needed to keep people safe and secure."

–ICE Assistant Secretary John Morton, January 2010[33]

"The clothes I was wearing I took off my clothes and gave to them, and they gave us the prisoner's uniform, a green uniform. Our hands were handcuffed and our ankles were tied. I couldn't tell what was day and what was night—there were no windows, and 24 hours light. It was hard to find out what was the time. It was very loud in my room, all the time, 48 detainees, and I could not escape it —I wanted to stay alone."

–Nepalese asylum seeker detained in 2011 in an immigration detention facility in Virginia

Despite these commitments from DHS and ICE two years ago, asylum seekers and other immigration detainees today are still overwhelmingly held in jails and jail-like facilities. In these facilities, they wear color-coded prison uniforms and live in conditions that are characteristic of penal facilities—their freedom of movement and outdoor access are highly limited; they often visit with friends and loved ones separated by Plexiglas barriers; and they have little or no privacy in toilets and showers. They are subject to multiple daily head counts, and they often have limited access to programming and must eat their meals in their housing units. These very conditions have led even prison experts, as well as the Inter-American Commission on Human Rights, to conclude that immigration detention facilities are essentially jails.[34]

In July 2009, approximately 50 percent of the ICE's population was held in actual correctional facilities that also held criminal detainees.[35] Since DHS and ICE announced intentions to reform the detention system, there has been no decrease in that proportion.[36] In fact, according to Human Rights First calculations, ICE has entered into agreements that will add 2,778 jail and jail-like beds to the system. (Those new bed locations are listed in the box on page 11.) And most of the remaining 50 percent of ICE immigration detainees—those who are not held in actual jails or prisons—are still held in jail-like facilities.[37] Furthermore, ICE uses the same facilities it was using in 2009, and under the same management. While ICE did indicate that the shift to a less penal system would take place "in three to five years,"[38] two years in, there is still a long way to go.

In 2010 and 2011, Human Rights First researchers visited 17 ICE-authorized detention facilities that together held more than 10,000 of the 33,400 total ICE beds.[39] These facilities included ICE-operated Service Processing Centers, privately operated Contract Detention Facilities, and county jails and prisons operating under Intergovernmental Service Agreements with ICE. The majority of the detainees at these facilities had no criminal history or only a non-violent criminal history.[40] In total, at the time of our visits the 17 facilities held hundreds of asylum seekers, as well as thousands of other immigrants in removal proceedings. Nearly all of these facilities looked like jails, operated like jails, and in many cases were actual jails.

These facilities are typically surrounded by multiple perimeter fences topped with razor wire, barbed wire, or concertina coils. They have a range of conditions that are identical or similar to those in criminal correctional facilities, including:

Prison uniforms: At these facilities, asylum seekers and other immigration detainees wear prison uniforms or jumpsuits. These uniforms are generally color-coded to denote a custody classification—light blue for "low security," orange for "medium security," and red for "high security." In other facilities, the colors have no correlation to security classification; for example, at Hudson County Correctional Center in New Jersey, ICE detainees of all security levels wear lime-green jumpsuits to distinguish them from county inmates and U.S. Marshal detainees.

Housing layout: Detainees are often held in large units with rows of bunk beds, sometimes totaling 48 or 64 beds, or in double cells. They sleep on thin and narrow foam mattresses. They are locked into their units, and sometimes locked into their cells. The housing units themselves have concrete walls and floor, and are lit with bright overhead lights. Stainless steel tables and benches are bolted to the floor. The units are often noisy, and always lack privacy. Frequently, detainees receive their meals in the same large room where they sleep and wash, meaning that they typically remain in that location constantly, except for a single hour of access to outdoor recreation that is required by detention standards.[41] When they do have access to a cafeteria, detainees must eat at specific times and have limited food options. The design of some facilities precludes exit from the housing area even for recreation. For example, at Hudson County Correctional Center in New Jersey, the "indoor/outdoor" recreation in the women's housing unit consists of a triangular space at one corner of a 64-person dormitory, open to the air through one wall of fencing, but technically indoors. On the day of our visit, the space contained one chin-up bar and a soccer ball that detainees were not permitted to use. The warden told us that they were waiting for delivery of a Nerf ball.

Highly restricted movement: As noted above, asylum seekers and other immigration detainees in these facilities are generally required to spend all or most of the day in their housing units. They are not permitted to access outdoor areas, medical services, a cafeteria, or the law library freely throughout the day. When they are

> *"A lady security officer at the entrance of the detention obliged me to take a shower so that I could dress up as a detainee, but the place that I took the shower was not covered and she could see me entirely and [she was] laughing very discreetly ... I could feel myself without privacy in that place. ... The bathrooms were open and covered with the mechanic eyes of cameras.... I was forced to prevent myself from relieving in those bathrooms in front the eyes in the day times."*
>
> –Refugee from Democratic Republic of Congo detained in 2010 at Elizabeth Detention Center in New Jersey

allowed to leave their housing unit, their access to other areas of the facility is typically very limited (such as a one-hour window for outdoor recreation each day), and at almost all facilities they must be escorted by guards or corrections officers—regardless of their criminal history or lack thereof—whether they are walking to the outdoor recreation area, the medical unit to meet with a nurse, to the law library to utilize one of the five hours they are permitted there each week, or to the cafeteria during mealtime, all destinations located within the secure facility. Detainees are generally subject to head counts up to eight times per day.

Lack of privacy in showers and toilets: Detainees are afforded limited to no privacy in showers and toilets. Sometimes, showers and toilets (often stainless steel toilets without seats) are not even separated by partial dividers or curtains; this was the case at Willacy Detention Center and Port Isabel Detention Center in Texas, El Centro Service Processing Center in California, and ICA-Farmville in Virginia, at the time of our tours.

Lack of true outdoor recreation: In some facilities, detainees do not have meaningful access to the outdoors, despite ICE's expectation "that every ICE/DRO detainee will be placed in a facility that provides indoor and outdoor recreation... [except] in exceptional circumstances."[42] In many facilities—including the Elizabeth Detention Center and Essex County and Hudson County jails in New Jersey, Tacoma Northwest Detention Center in Washington, and Pinal County jail in Arizona[43]—the "outdoor" recreation is not actually outdoors at all; instead it is a concrete room with high ceilings and small windows or fencing at the top to allow some air and light to enter, or one triangular corner of the housing unit open to the air only through a wall of fencing. Baker County jail in Florida does not have outdoor recreation at all. In other facilities, the outdoor recreation area is actually outdoors, but it lacks the kind of shade necessary to protect detainees from the intense sunlight and heat in many areas where these facilities are located; in late June 2011, when we visited El Centro, in southern California just 15 miles from the border with Mexico, during outdoor recreation time many detainees were crouched against the wall in the limited shade to find some relief from the intense sun and 100-degree heat.

Limited outdoor recreation hours: The detention standards require detainees to receive just one hour of recreation per day, outdoors if possible.[44] In practice, many facilities do not exceed this standard—and even those that do generally permit only two or three additional hours[45]—so for up to 23 hours each day, detainees may be required to remain inside their housing unit, which is often noisy, lacking natural light, and completely lacking in privacy.

No contact visits: In many facilities, also regardless of criminal history or lack thereof, detainees can visit with their family and friends for just 30 minutes at a time, only on specific days of the week, and only via telephone, sitting across from each other, separated by glass or Plexiglas dividers.[46] Even worse, in some facilities, "visits" take place only via video, even when visitors are in the same building as detainees, including at Pinal County Jail (Arizona), which houses more than 400 men. Detainees at Pinal County are not permitted contact visits even with their attorneys.[47] Other facilities that permit visits only via video include Douglas County Corrections (127 detainees), Baker County jail (250 detainees),

Port Isabel Detention Center in Harlingen, Texas, holds 850 ICE detainees.

Etowah County jail (349 detainees), Ramsey County Adult Detention Center (66 detainees), McHenry County Correctional Facility (315 detainees), Sherburne County jail (115 detainees), Freeborn County jail (75 detainees), and Jack Harwell Detention Facility (in September 2011, ICE increased its bed use at Jack Harwell by about 100).[48] In only a few facilities can detainees greet their family members or other visitors with a hug, and sit side by side as they visit with each other—while monitored by officers or guards.[49]

Lack of programming: Most facilities provide little or no activities or programming for detainees held in their custody—despite the view of many corrections professionals that a lack of activities for otherwise idle inmates or detainees can actually undermine the safety of a facility.[50] Aside from one hour of recreation—in a space that may or may not have exercise or sports equipment—detainees generally sit in their housing units all day, watching television, playing cards, talking, or sleeping. Indeed, at Hudson County jail in New Jersey, when we toured the women's dormitory around 11 am, at least a dozen women were lying in their beds, listless, and still wearing pajamas

After surveying the conditions at 19 facilities used by ICE, a prison expert retained by the U.S. Commission on International Religious Freedom concluded in 2005 that these facilities "in most critical respects...are structured and operated much like standardized correctional facilities," resembling, "in every essential respect, conventional jails."[51] In 2009, ICE itself acknowledged that the agency's detention beds "are spread out over as many as 350 different facilities largely designed for penal, not civil, detention," and that current detention practices are "jail-oriented."[52] In the DHS-ICE 2009 report, Dr. Schriro confirmed that "[a]ll but a few of the facilities that ICE uses to detain aliens were built as jails and prisons."[53] These jails and jail-like facilities—whose conditions reflect more restrictions than necessary[54]—are inappropriately penal for a population detained under civil immigration laws.

Not only have U.S. government reports and prison experts concluded that these prison-like conditions are inappropriate for asylum seekers and immigration detainees, but these conditions are also inconsistent with U.S. commitments under the Refugee Convention, its Protocol, and the International Covenant on Civil and Political Rights. When migrants and asylum seekers are subjected to administrative detention, they should be held in conditions that are non-punitive and non-penal and that take into account their needs and their status as administrative, not criminal law, detainees.[55] In a December 2010 report, the Inter-American Commission on Human Rights affirmed that "the conditions of [immigration] detention ought not to be punitive or prisonlike," and stressed its concern "that this principle is not observed in immigration detention in the United States."[56] In a March 2008 report, the UN Special Rapporteur on the Human Rights of Migrants expressed concern about the punitive and "prison-like" nature of detention for immigration detainees in the United States, concluding that "[t]he conditions and terms of their detention are often prison-like: freedom of movement is restricted and detainees wear prison uniforms and are kept in a punitive setting."[57]

Only three of the 254 existing facilities used by ICE (reduced from 350 since 2009) have conditions that might be considered less penal—Broward Transitional Center in Florida, T. Don Hutto Residential Center in Texas, and Berks Family Detention Center in Pennsylvania. (These facilities are described in detail beginning on page 35.) ICE has touted these facilities as models, either in whole or in part, for a civil detention system,[58] but together they hold just 1,137 detainees—between 3 and 4 percent of ICE's total detained population.[59] The vast majority of detained asylum seekers and other immigrants continue to be held in jails and jail-like facilities.

Since its 2009 reform announcements, ICE has entered into contracts that will add 2,778 jail beds to the immigration detention system (as well as beds at several less penal facilities, which are discussed beginning on page 18). These facilities include:

Adelanto, CA—1,300 new jail-like beds: In June 2011, ICE announced that it had entered into a contract with Adelanto, to house detainees in an existing "correctional facility" that was purchased by GEO Group from the city of Adelanto in June 2010.[60] The contract had been signed the month before. According to news reports, GEO Group had proposed as early as September 2009 that the site be used by ICE to detain immigrants.[61] The facility, which has 650 beds, began to house ICE detainees in August 2011.[62] GEO Group will add 650 more beds for ICE's use by August 2012.[63] The contract between ICE and Adelanto, obtained by Human Rights First through a public information request, contains no indication that conditions at this facility will be any different from the standard jail-like conditions at existing ICE-authorized facilities. It will be inspected against the corrections-based 2008 Performance-Based National Detention Standards.[64] Adelanto is 85 miles from Los Angeles.

Essex County, NJ—300 new jail beds: In August 2011, ICE announced that it had entered into a contract with Essex County that would expand existing ICE bed space at Essex County Correctional Facility by 300 beds, from 500 to 800.[65] (It would also create 450 new beds at Delaney Hall with somewhat less penal conditions.) Essex County jail also houses more than 1,500 detainees for the county and for the U.S. Marshals Service. It is impossible to distinguish them from the ICE detainees, but for the lime-green jumpsuits worn by ICE detainees. At present, detainees at Essex do not have access to the actual outdoors; the recreation space is a small interior cement-floor "courtyard" with openings to the sky in each dormitory, or cement-floor courtyards abutting the dormitories. Detainees are housed in units of 48 to 64 beds, and eat their meals in their dormitories; they cannot leave unless they are scheduled for a medical appointment or a visit to the law library (which is long out of date, and contains no law dictionary that would assist a detainee in preparing a case pro se). Detainees are guarded by County officers, not ICE officers.[66] The new

SINCE 2009—NEW ICE BEDS

To date, ICE has entered tentatively or formally into agreements for the following new or expanded facilities, adding a total of 6,360 beds to the system after the planned facilities are up and running.

- Adelanto, CA: 1,300-bed facility owned, retrofitted, and operated by GEO Group (IGSA)—opened August 2011

- Aurora, CO—97-bed expansion at Denver Contract Detention Facility, operated by GEO Group (CDF)—new contract announced September 2011[67]

- Crete, IL: 700-bed facility designed and operated by Corrections Corporation of America (IGSA) - proposed

- Essex County, NJ: 300-bed expansion at Essex County jail and 450-bed addition at Delaney Hall, operated by Community Education Centers (IGSA)—opened October 2011

- Henderson, NV: 196 new beds at Henderson Detention Center, operated by Henderson Police Division—increased ICE beds February 2011

- Karnes County, TX: 600-bed facility designed and operated by GEO Group (IGSA)—scheduled to open early 2012

- Ocilla, GA: 295 beds at Irwin County Detention Center, managed by Michael Croft Enterprises (IGSA) —increased ICE beds September 2010

- Orange County, CA: 235 beds at James A. Musick Facility in Irvine and 587 beds at Theo Lacy in Santa Ana, operated by Orange County police department (IGSA)—opened June 2010[68]

- Southwest Ranches, FL: 1,500- to 2,000-bed facility designed and operated by Corrections Corporation of America (IGSA)—proposed

- Waco, TX: 100 new beds at Jack Harwell Detention Center, operated by Community Education Centers (IGSA) - increased ICE beds September 2011

In October 2011, senior ICE officials advised Human Rights First that: "One of the agency's goals in adding detention beds in particular regions has been to reduce the need for transfers of detainees from the areas where they are apprehended and are more likely to have family members, attorneys, and ongoing immigration proceedings. That goal has been achieved in two regions where transfers were a particular problem—Los Angeles and the Northeast. Transfers of detainees, prior to their final orders of removal, from the Los Angeles Field Office have decreased from 79% and 71% of total external transfers in FY09 and FY10, respectively, to 33% in FY11 through August, and the total number of external transfers has also decreased substantially. Similar, transfers from the New York City Field Office have also decreased steadily as new detention beds have been added there in recent months. These trends are expected to continue as detention capacity is added in those areas. This increased local capacity, however, has not had the effect of increasing the total number of detention beds ICE utilizes nationwide."[69] To date, ICE has publicly ended the active use of just one facility—the Willacy Detention Center in Texas.[70] ICE has not announced any other plans to close existing facilities that are currently housing detainees.

contract requires some modifications to the existing conditions—true outdoor recreation within one year, contact visits within 30 days, and uniforms that "conform to the civil detention objectives of ICE"[71]—but these changes would not change the fact that the facility is a jail. Essex County jail is in Newark.

Henderson, NV—196 new jail beds: In February 2011, ICE increased its bed space at the Henderson Detention Center from 19 to 80. As of July 2011, it has 215 beds available for ICE detainees.[72] The facility—which also holds Henderson misdemeanants, U.S. Marshals Service inmates, U.S. Park Service, Clark County inmates, and Boulder City Police Department misdemeanor arrestees—

is run by the City of Henderson Police Division.[73] Henderson is 15 miles from Las Vegas.

Ocilla, GA—295 new jail beds: In September 2010, ICE received approval to use the Irwin County Detention Center in Ocilla, which is managed by Michael Croft Enterprises for Irwin County's sheriff's department, as a facility to hold detainees for more than 72 hours.[74] As of July 2011, the facility has 295 beds available for ICE detainees.[75] Ocilla is 180 miles from Atlanta and 110 miles from Tallahassee.

Orange County, CA—587 new jail beds: In July 2010, ICE finalized a contract with Orange County to hold immigration detainees at two existing correctional facilities. As of July 2011, ICE had access to 235 at the

James A. Musick Detention Facility in Irvine and 587 at Theo Lacy in Santa Ana.[76] Musick offers some less penal conditions, but at Theo Lacy, contact visits are not permitted, and ICE detainees have no freedom of movement, and no privacy in showers or toilets. In one area of the facility, detainees do not have access to true outdoor recreation.[77] Santa Ana is 34 miles from Los Angeles.

Waco, TX—100 new jail beds: In early September 2011, legal service providers and visitation programs in central Texas began to hear rumors that ICE was housing detainees at the Jack Harwell Detention Center in Waco. The facility had been built for McLellan County by a private prison company called Community Education Centers. When it opened in 2010, Jack Harwell was described as a "jail" by the *Waco Tribune*.[78] Legal service providers had never visited the facility, which according to ICE data has been approved to house detainees for less than 72 hours. On September 19, local ICE informed one legal service provider in Austin that ICE was now holding about 100 female detainees at Jack Harwell.[79] Waco is 104 miles from Austin and 98 miles from Dallas

Since its reform announcements two years ago, the government has not only continued to use jails and jail-like facilities to detain asylum seekers and other immigration detainees; it has also increased the number of jail and jail-like beds available across the country for ICE detainees by 2,778. While these new beds may ultimately decrease the number of detainee transfers—which in turn would reduce separation of families, loss of legal representation, and other hardships that have resulted from high transfer levels in recent years[80]—they do not move DHS and ICE toward its promised shift away from penal facilities to facilities with conditions more appropriate for civil immigration detainees.

Immigration Detention Costs U.S. Taxpayers Over $2 Billion

"[Present immigration detention] standards impose more restrictions and carry more costs than are necessary to effectively manage the majority of the detained population."

–2009 DHS-ICE report[81]

"Utilizing a variety of small local jails increases cost and transportation needs."

–DHS-ICE ten-year strategic plan, 2003[82]

The costs of immigration detention have skyrocketed in recent years, with U.S. immigration authorities detaining an increasing number of individuals and holding them in several hundred jails and jail-like facilities across the country. Since 2005, ICE has **increased the number of beds it uses to detain immigrants by 67 percent**.[83] In 2010 alone, ICE detained approximately 363,000 asylum seekers and other immigrants—a 53 percent increase since 2005, when that number was 238,000.[84] In its budget request for fiscal year 2012, DHS asked Congress for $2.02 billion to cover the costs of maintaining bed space and other needs associated with detaining immigrants. In FY 2005, the same budget line was $864 million[85]. Over seven years, then, the U.S. government has **increased its spending on detention bed space by 134 percent.** ICE projects that for FY 2012 it will pay an average of **$122 per day per detainee.**[86] Congress plays a key role in maintaining and increasing the number of available immigration detention beds by explicitly authorizing ICE to maintain immigration detention bed space, and reliably increasing its funding for these beds every year.

At an average daily cost of $122, American taxpayers are funding the detention of up to 33,400 immigration detainees on any given day—and a total of almost 400,000 each year. The average detainee length of stay is 30 days[87] - but 38 percent of detainees are deported or released within one week, so a large proportion of individuals remain in detention for much longer than 30 days. According to the most recent data that ICE has made available (from 2008), the average length of stay

for detained asylum seekers is 102.4 days—and some are held for up to a year or longer.[88] Based on ICE's own daily cost information,[89] Human Rights First estimates that the government pays more than $3,500 to detain an asylum seeker or other immigration detainee for 30 days, more than $12,000 for 102 days, and more than $43,000 to detain one asylum seeker or other immigration detainee in the current system for a year.

LENGTH OF DETENTION	COST
2 weeks	$1,708
1 month	$3,660
3 months	$10,980
6 months	$21,960
1 year	$43,920

DHS and ICE have pledged repeatedly that their detention reform efforts will be budget-neutral—they will spend more in some areas, save money in others, and ultimately come out even. DHS's October 6 fact sheet detailed the ways that each category of reform should save money, for example through developing facilities commensurate to risk, expanding Alternatives to Detention, and reducing detainee transfers.[90] Secretary Napolitano positioned ICE's planned reforms as an effort to "ensure that we [detain] in the most cost-effective way possible."[91] In fact, effective reforms to the U.S. immigration detention system could result in cost-savings to U.S. taxpayers, and these reforms could be implemented without sacrificing the safety of detainees, officers, or the public.

First, detention costs can be reduced by limiting or ending detention that is unnecessary. For example, current Alternatives to Detention cost on average $8.88 per day[92]—more than $110 less per day than detention. As detailed beginning on page 26, Alternatives to Detention—which generally provide for release from immigration detention with some additional measures to monitor the individual after release—are provided to ICE under a new consolidated contract with BI Incorporated, a private company owned by the publicly traded prison contractor GEO Group. ICE places Alternatives to Detention enrollees into one of two programs—a "full-service" program with "intensive case management, supervision, electronic monitoring, and individuals service plans," or a "technology-only" program that uses GPS tracking and phone reporting. In 2010, 93 percent of individuals actively enrolled in these programs attended their final court hearings, and 84 percent complied with removal orders.[93] Prior Alternatives to Detention programs have also confirmed substantial costs savings along with high appearance rates.[94] Nevertheless, for fiscal year 2012, DHS requested $2.02 billion for its detention budget—28 times its $72.4 million request to fund Alternatives to Detention.[95]

Second, as several experts and government officials have emphasized, shifting from a corrections model to a less penal model of detention should ultimately prove less costly. In the 2009 DHS-ICE report, Dr. Schriro affirmed that "[present immigration detention] standards impose more restrictions and *carry more costs than are necessary to effectively manage the majority of the detained population*."[96] DHS Secretary Napolitano has similarly acknowledged that jail-like conditions can lead to unnecessary expenses. At an October 2009 press conference, she noted that the current immigration detention system "is a system that encompasses many different types of detainees, not all of whom need to be held in prison-like circumstances or jail-like circumstances which not only may be unnecessary but more expensive than necessary."[97] The former Secretary of the California Department of Corrections and former warden of San Quentin State Prison Jeanne Woodford has confirmed that "a system that classifies adult detainees appropriately at the lowest security level possible, provides maximum freedom of movement to detainees according to their custody classification level, and utilizes modern technology to supplement staffing *will ultimately reduce costs*."[98] Even ten years ago, the then-new DHS recognized that "[u]tilizing a variety of small local jails increases cost and transportation needs."[99] Half of all detainees today are still held in local jails. An immigration detention system dependent on jails is not cost-effective.

Same Detention Standards

"ICE has continued to implement major reforms to our immigration detention system, [including] drafting new detention standards…"

  –DHS Secretary Janet Napolitano, March 2011

"The problem with the existing standards that we have is that they are based on the American Correctional Association standards. They are largely coming out of the penal world, and that's not where I want to be. I want us to be in an immigration detention world."

  –ICE Assistant Secretary John Morton, January 2010

"Establishing standards for Immigration Detention is our challenge and our opportunity."

  –DHS-ICE report, October 2009[100]

When ICE committed in 2009 to move away from a "jail-oriented approach to a system wholly designed for and based on ICE's civil detention authorities,"[101] the agency promised to develop new detention standards that would "reflect the new environment" and conditions appropriate for civil immigration detention populations. Assistant Secretary Morton announced, "We are going to move to new standards that reflect the new environment and the new programs and practices."[102] He also stressed that "[w]e all need to work together so that in a few years we will have standards for what I hope is going to be an entirely new world."[103] A DHS fact sheet on the reforms promised to "[r]evise immigration detention standards to reflect the conditions appropriate for various immigration detainee populations" by the end of FY 2010.[104] In testimony before Congress in 2011, Secretary Napolitano said that ICE was "drafting new detention standards" as part of its detention reform efforts.[105] Dr. Schriro recommended that ICE "[d]evelop and adopt civil detention standards and operating procedures consistent with civil detention."[106]

Such standards—specific to civil detention—would provide some measure of accountability for ICE and for contractors or local government staff operating ICE-authorized facilities. The American Correctional Association states that standards "are necessary to ensure that correctional facilities are operated professionally."[107] The former American Bar Association president Martha Barnett has called standards a good first step toward "providing uniform treatment… for immigrants and asylum-seekers."[108] In addition to helping ensure professional and consistent reforms, new civil standards would also serve to spell out ICE's expectations in detail for the officials on the ground operating the facilities on a daily basis. During Human Rights First's tour of El Centro Service Processing Center in California, one local official said that that staff and officers are "very standards and compliance oriented." He added, "If [leadership] told us to do it, we'd make it happen."[109] At Port Isabel Service Processing Center in Texas, the ICE assistant field office director reported to us that ICE headquarters had indicated plans to shift to a "softer and lighter" detention model, but had issued no specific guidance.[110]

Yet two years after its reform promises, ICE has not developed or implemented new standards for the new environment and conditions appropriate for civil immigration detention. Just as they were in 2009, immigration detention facilities are still inspected according to two different sets of detention standards, the 2000 National Detention Standards (NDS) or the 2008 Performance-Based National Detention Standards

(PBNDS), depending on the facility.[111] Both of these sets of standards are based on the American Correctional Association's standards for adult local detention facilities. The 2009 DHS-ICE report confirmed: "ICE relies primarily on correctional incarceration standards designed for pre-trial felons and on correctional principles of care, custody, and control." The report concluded that "[t]hese standards impose more restrictions... than are necessary to effectively manage the majority of the detained population."[112] In USCIRF's 2005 report, its prison expert drew a similar conclusion: "[B]oth the letter and spirit of the DRO [ICE's Detention and Removal Operations division] detention standards appear to embody a traditional correctional system approach.... These standards clearly model those in use in traditional prisons and jails...."[113] In January 2010, ICE Assistant Secretary Morton agreed: "The problem with the existing standards that we have is that they are based on the American Correctional Association Standards. They are largely coming out of the penal world and that's not where I want to be."[114]

In the 2009 DHS-ICE report, Dr. Schriro recommended that discussions among stakeholders with respect to the drafting of detention standards and operating procedures should "focus on the underlying assumptions that inform operating decisions about movement, meal service, housing, dress, visitation, work, and worship, among other important daily activities."[115] ICE has outlined some key elements of the environment and conditions that would "ideally" be included in "a wholly new generation of detention facilities uniquely suited to ICE's civil detention authority" in a "Statement of Objectives" (SOO) for detention reform. The SOO was prepared in order to solicit concept proposals for new facilities throughout the country.[116] (A copy of the SOO appears as an appendix to this report.)

The DHS-ICE Statement of Objectives describes various conditions the agency wants to see in new facilities, including those relating to movement, meal service, housing, dress, visitation and worship—the same kinds of factors that were identified in the DHS-ICE report in connection with the drafting of immigration detention standards. For example, the SOO soliciting a new facility in Florida calls for "ideally, a minimum of four hours per day of outdoor recreation ... in a natural setting that allows for vigorous aerobic exercise," contact visitation, and "non-institutional detainee clothing and staff uniforms." These are the kinds of matters that are typically addressed in standards. However, ICE's current detention standards do not require facilities to provide the conditions described in the Statement of Objectives. Rather—for example—current standards assure immigration detainees just one hour of outdoor access each day, require detainees to wear institutional uniforms, and leave contact visits up to the discretion of the facility operator.[117]

As things stand now, any new facilities—and the private prison companies and county sheriff's departments that operate these facilities—will have no new standards they must commit to complying with. Instead, new "civil detention" facilities such as the GEO Group facility being constructed in Karnes County, will be inspected against the existing corrections-based standards.[118] Moreover, applying the current standards to new facilities could cause significant confusion, undermining efforts to reform the system, since the current standards—as noted above—describe greater restrictions than those contemplated by ICE's own Statement of Objectives for new facilities. ICE's SOOs do indicate that "Adult Residential Standards" were "under development" at some point in 2010, and would apply to so-called "non-secure" beds.[119] But ICE's new contracts with Karnes County (Texas), Orange County (California), and Essex County (New Jersey)—for facilities designed to provide less penal conditions—still require compliance with the existing PBNDS 2008 and do not reference Adult Residential Standards.[120]

In October 2011, senior ICE officials advised Human Rights First that:

> ICE has also drafted a revised version of its national detention standards, referred to more commonly as the 2011 Performance-Based National Detention Standards (PBNDS). Once published, the 2011 PBNDS will supersede the earlier Performance-Based National Standards that were issued in September 2008. These standards are now undergoing Union review. The new 2011 standards were developed in close consultation with the agency's advisory groups and with DHS CRCL. The 2011 standards will be more tailored to the unique needs of ICE's detained population, as they maximize access to counsel, visitation, religious practices, and recreation, while improving the agency's prevention and response to sexual abuse or

assault that may occur in detention facilities and strengthening standards for quality medical, mental health, and dental care.[121]

In fact, NGOs have not reviewed these revised standards, and saw an earlier version in June 2010 only after it was leaked to a reporter at the *Houston Chronicle*. At that time, the revisions did not maximize access to things like outdoor recreation, but instead provided a range of acceptable outcomes, from minimal to optimal; in the case of outdoor recreation, for example, the minimum requirement was one hour, and the optimal requirement was four hours, with no apparent incentive for facilities to attain optimal compliance.

The American Bar Association, which has played a leading role since the 1990s in advocating for standards for U.S. facilities that hold immigration detainees, is currently drafting model standards that will outline some of the key conditions that should exist in "civil" immigration detention facilities, including standards relating to appropriate dress, outdoor access, movement within facilities and facility grounds, and contact visits.

The importance of standards to ensure accountability and compliance at U.S. immigration detention centers has been recognized repeatedly over the years, including by DHS Deputy Secretary Jane Holl Lute, who affirmed in July 2009 that detention standards "promote best practices and accountability" and "facilitate oversight of facilities."[122] Former ICE Assistant Secretary Julie L. Myers also affirmed in 2008 that "standards allow us to meet our solemn responsibility to all those in our custody."[123] In 2003, the new agency's ten-year strategic plan stated: "Detention and Removal Operations [responsible for ICE's detention operations] acknowledges that nationwide operations cannot be conducted consistently without unified operations plans and clear guidance to

the field." It listed "codes, regulations, and standards" as key mechanisms to ensure compliance.[124] A range of other experts on corrections and immigration detention have echoed this assertion.[125] In the absence of new standards, ICE should incorporate its SOO into all new facility contracts, and commit to actually utilize sanctions for contract noncompliance. This approach would be appropriate in the immediate to short term, but it is not an effective or appropriate substitute for standards over the longer term.

Promulgation of detention standards for correctional facilities in the 1970s and 1980s was an important step forward for reform of prison conditions across the United States.[126] As they take steps to transform the civil immigration detention system, DHS and ICE should likewise develop new civil detention standards for "a system wholly designed for and based on ICE's civil detention authorities."[127] Most of ICE's existing facilities—particularly the jails, which comprise 50 percent of ICE beds—would not be able to comply with civil detention standards based on ICE's own principles described in their Statement of Objectives, or based on the recommendations outlined in this report. To effect the transformation it has promised, ICE would need to phase out the use of facilities that could not comply with civil detention standards, except for the small percentage of the detained population that might pose a danger to other detainees or officers unless held in jail-like conditions. The agency would also need to ensure that its on-site monitors as well as its data systems could collect the information necessary to assess standards compliance—a recommendation described in detail in 2009 by the Migration Policy Institute[128]—and be willing to utilize sanctions for noncompliance.

Some Steps Forward on Shift to Less Penal Conditions

Since its reform announcements in fall 2009, ICE has taken some steps toward the shift away from penal conditions for immigration law detainees. The steps—which are outlined directly below—include plans for several facilities that are anticipated to offer conditions less penal than those in the majority of existing ICE facilities, as well as minor improvements at some existing jail-like ICE facilities.

New less penal beds

According to various statements and reports, ICE is in the process of planning or opening five new detention facilities that will reflect the kind of conditions outlined in its Statement of Objectives. If the planned facilities open as scheduled, ICE would potentially have about 3,485 new beds in facilities with less penal conditions—though these facilities would also retain some significant penal elements. These new beds, along with the 1,137 beds that ICE already uses in several existing facilities with less penal conditions, would mean that ICE would have a total of 4,622 beds in less penal facilities. These 4,622 beds would comprise 14 percent of ICE's detained asylum seeker and immigrant population—meaning that 86 percent of ICE detainees would still be held in jail and jail-like facilities.

These new planned facilities include:

Crete, IL—700 less penal beds: In June 2011, ICE tentatively accepted a proposal for a 700-bed facility in Crete, to be built and operated by Corrections Corporation of America (CCA) on a site to be acquired by CCA in Crete. In response to an inquiry from Human Rights First about the planned Crete facility, senior ICE officials stated: "As reflected in the Statement of Objectives for both facilities, ICE expects that the substantially improved conditions of detention will apply to all detainees at Southwest Ranches and Crete, including the majority of detainees that will be medium and high-risk. The agency expects that these improvements will include free movement to and from outside recreation for at least four hours a day; enhanced programming; enhance law library and legal resources;

contact visitation; natural ambient light throughout the facility; dedicated space for religious services; cafeteria-style meal service; and non-institutional clothing."[129] ICE, Crete, and CCA have not come to a final agreement on the project, and its timeline was redacted from the materials obtained by Human Rights First.[130] Crete is 40 miles from Chicago.

Essex County, NJ—450 less penal beds: In August 2011, ICE announced that it had entered into a contract with Essex County that would create 450 new beds in somewhat less penal conditions at an existing substance abuse treatment facility, Delaney Hall, operated by the private company Community Education Centers.[131] (The contract also expands ICE bed space at Essex County jail from 500 to 800.) Delaney Hall's less penal elements include dorm-style eight-person rooms, some freedom of movement within the ICE wing of the facility, spacious common areas, and abundant natural light. Detainees would be permitted contact visits and controlled email access, and would wear t-shirts and khaki pants.[132] In early October, however, during the first few days of operation, ICE detainees at Delaney were wearing lime-green prison jumpsuits.[133] The outdoor recreation area attached to the facility lacks shade and grass, and is sometimes plagued with foul smells emanating from the meat-rendering plant next door or the sewage treatment plant less than a mile away.[134] The contract between ICE and Essex County contains contradictory information about outdoor access at Delaney Hall; in various locations, it promises six hours per day, more than six hours per day, and more than seven hours per day. The access is not open, however; the contract prescribes that "movement between recreation, housing, and programs will occur on 30 minute intervals." Delaney Hall is located across the parking lot from Essex County jail in Newark.

Karnes County, TX—600 less penal beds: In December 2010, ICE signed a contract for a new 600-bed facility in Karnes County that ICE called "the first of its kind." The private contractor GEO Group called the facility "the first Civil Detention Center for immigration detainees in the United States."[135] It is explicitly intended to house "Level

1 detainees that include non-criminals as well as individuals with very minor, non-violent criminal records." The contract requires that the facility offer a number of conditions, including: [136]

- "reasonable freedom of detainee movement within the walls while at the same time controlling the ability of detainees to walk away from the facility"

- detainees "may be dressed in relaxed, non-traditional clothing"

- perimeter walls rather than "fences, razor, or barbed wire"

- true outdoor recreation area with exercise equipment

- potential for extended outdoor recreation hours[137]

- individual rooms for up to 8 detainees

- private bathrooms and showers

- contact visitation

- multipurpose rooms for indoor activities

- separate cafeteria

- potential for Internet access under "very controlled access" to maintain family ties[138]

- potential for programming

- facility staff "may be dressed in non-traditional uniforms such as khaki pants and polo shirts"

- staff "may be provided" with training related to "communication skills, sensitivity, [and] multi-cultural awareness"

- "ample" natural light.

This facility is projected to open in February 2012. Karnes County is 60 miles from San Antonio, and 100 miles from Austin.

Orange County, CA—235 less penal beds: In July 2010, ICE finalized its contract with Orange County to hold immigrant detainees at two existing correctional facilities. As of July 2011, ICE had access to 235 beds at the James A. Musick Detention Facility in Irvine.[139] At Musick, ICE detainees—who wear "wine"-colored prison uniforms—are permitted to move freely among their housing unit, the outdoor recreation area, the law library, and the cafeteria (during scheduled mealtimes lasting no more than 15 minutes), except during head counts, which

take place 7 times per day. They can receive contact visits. Musick is subject to the 2008 PBNDS, which are based on correctional standards, and the IGSA between ICE and Orange County states that the "types and levels of services [for ICE detainees] shall be consistent with those the Service Provider [Orange County] routinely affords other inmates"—namely, criminal inmates in the Orange County Sheriff Department's custody.[140] Even with this provision, ICE detainees at Musick have access to fewer programming and work opportunities than do the criminal inmates held at the facility. Irvine is 40 miles from Los Angeles.

Southwest Ranches, FL—1,500 less penal beds: In June 2011, ICE tentatively accepted a proposal for a 1,500-bed facility in Southwest Ranches, Florida. The facility would be built on land already owned by the Corrections Corporation of America.[141] In response to an inquiry from Human Rights First about the planned Southwest Ranches facility, senior ICE officials stated: "As reflected in the Statement of Objectives for both facilities, ICE expects that the substantially improved conditions of detention will apply to all detainees at Southwest Ranches and Crete, including the majority of detainees that will be medium and high-risk. The agency expects that these improvements will include free movement to and from outside recreation for at least four hours a day; enhanced programming; enhance law library and legal resources; contact visitation; natural ambient light throughout the facility; dedicated space for religious services; cafeteria-style meal service; and non-institutional clothing."[142] ICE, Southwest Ranches, and CCA have not come to a final agreement on the plan, which will also require approval from the Broward County Commission. The proposal estimates that design and construction would take 18 to 24 months.[143] Southwest Ranches is 30 miles from Miami.

ICE considers the Karnes County facility in Texas and Delaney Hall in New Jersey to be "templates" for new stand-alone civil detention facilities. However these templates—at least as currently planned—continue to retain some conditions that could be described as penal. For instance, while detained asylum seekers and immigrants at these facilities will not wear traditional prison jumpsuits, they will not be allowed to wear their own clothing, and will instead be required to wear facility-issued uniform clothing. (In the first few days of operation at Delaney, in fact, ICE detainees were actually wearing lime-green prison jumpsuits.) In addition, the facilities still propose to limit outdoor access for detainees, and in the case of Delaney Hall, detainees will be allowed to move from one location to another within the facility only on the half hour. Other models—like Berks, Hutto, and Broward Detention Center—provide outdoor access throughout the day.

Overall, as detailed in the box on page 11, ICE plans to add 6,360 new beds to the system. The facilities listed above, which would provide less penal conditions than existing jails and jail-like facilities, comprise 3,485 of those new beds. According to at least one news report, federal immigration officials have indicated their intent both to create new civil detention facilities *and* to close other detention facilities,"[144] but to date ICE has publicly ended the use of just one active facility—the Willacy Detention Center in Texas.[145] (That facility held 1,105 immigration detainees on the day that Human Rights First visited it.) ICE has not announced any other plans to close existing facilities that are currently housing detainees. The agency's proposals to add several thousand new beds to the system, without announcing concurrent plans to close any facilities, have triggered concerns relating to the further expansion of the flawed U.S. immigration detention system. (See page 22.)

Moreover, even at these new facilities with less penal conditions, detention can still be—and is—penal in nature when the detention itself runs afoul of other human rights protections—for example, when detention is not necessary, reasonable, or proportionate, or is unnecessarily prolonged.[146] And, as detailed beginning on page 26, the U.S. detention system still lacks a number of essential safeguards that would prevent detention from being arbitrary or otherwise inconsistent with U.S. obligations under the Refugee Convention and the International Covenant on Civil and Political Rights.

Improvements to existing beds

Some mostly minor improvements have been made at some existing jails and jail-like facilities over the past two years. ICE has not publicly reported on any changes to these facilities, but Human Rights First has identified some of these improvements through detention facility tours and interviews with local legal service providers and volunteers.

■   Contact visits are now reportedly available to detainees at facilities including Elizabeth Detention Center (New Jersey), Hudson County Jail (New Jersey), Monmouth County jail (New Jersey) (with advance permission), James A. Musick Facility (California), and ICA-Farmville (Virginia). Contact visits were available prior to ICE's reforms announcements at Port Isabel Detention Center (Texas) (with special request), Eloy Federal Contract Facility (Arizona) (though visitation space is insufficient for the volume of legal and non-legal visits), T. Don Hutto Residential Detention Center (Texas), Berks Family Residential Center (Pennsylvania), Broward Transitional Center (Florida), and Karnes County Correctional Center (Texas).[147]

■   At South Texas Detention Center (Texas), according to local ICE officials, over the past year visitation hours were increased by two hours per day, and expanded to three days each week from two. Law library hours were increased by two hours per day, and from five to seven days per week. The facility now has a "softer" paint scheme of yellows and greens. Detainees have access to new programming and activities.[148]

■   At Port Isabel Detention Center (Texas), the assistant field office director reported that the facility would open a new outdoor recreation space with a soccer field, two basketball half-courts, and a running track. He also promised that outdoor recreation would be expanded to two hours per day during the week. The facility has installed dividers between toilets for low- and medium-risk detainees.[149]

In May 2010, Corrections Corporation of America, a private prison contractor that runs nine ICE-only facilities holding almost 6,400 detainees (as well as holding the contracts to run four other correctional facilities used by ICE through IGSAs), reportedly agreed to make a number of changes at its ICE-only facilities. These changes included some freedom of movement and non-penal clothing for low-risk detainees, expanded programming, four hours' daily recreation time, elimination of lockdowns for low-risk detainees, expanded visitation time, contact visitation, email access, variety in the daily meals, fresh paint on the walls, normalized common areas, and available water and tea in the housing units at all times. These changes were to be implemented within six months.[150] As of October 2011—18 months later—the bulk of these reforms do not appear to have been implemented, and the conditions in the nine CCA facilities remain mostly penal in nature. We were able to confirm the following changes:[151]

- At Elizabeth Detention Center (New Jersey), the women's showers now have shower curtains. Contact visits are newly available to detainees. The walls have been painted sea-foam green, and the housing units have plants. In this jail-like facility, detained asylum seekers and immigrants still wear prison uniforms, lack freedom of movement within the facility, and have no meaningful outdoor access.

- At Eloy Federal Contract Facility, the women's housing areas have been painted in pastel colors.

- At Houston Contract Detention Facility, the walls have been painted.

- At San Diego Correctional Facility, one daytime count was eliminated, thus eliminating one daily lockdown. Detainees continue to wear prison uniforms, family visitation has not expanded, email remains unavailable, the walls have not been painted, and the common areas are still furnished with steel tables and chairs.

Challenges to Reform

Although U.S. immigration officials have repeatedly emphasized that facility safety and security are priorities of detention reform,[152] and multiple studies demonstrate that the planned reforms can actually help improve facility safety,[153] the ICE union has raised concerns about the reform's impact on officer and detainee safety. In June 2010, National ICE Council 118 of the American Federation of Government Employees, which represents 7,600 ICE employees, issued a vote of no confidence in ICE's Assistant Secretary Morton and the Assistant Director of ICE's Office of Detention Policy and Planning. The ICE union made a number of claims, including that the ICE leadership "dedicates more time to campaigning for immigration reforms aimed at large scale amnesty legislation than advising the American public and Federal lawmakers on the severity of the illegal immigration problem," does not request sufficient resources from Congress to detain and deport, and prohibits ICE officers from performing law enforcement duties. Council 118's vote also contended that ICE's detention reforms are "aimed at providing resort like living conditions to criminal aliens... with a priority of providing bingo nights, dance lessons and hanging plants to criminals, instead of addressing safe and responsible reforms for non-criminal individuals and families."[154] Council 118 President Chris Crane has asserted that the union is concerned about "ICE's plans to abandon vital security protocols currently in place in detention facilities, while intensifying efforts to arrest criminal aliens" and that these plans "will undoubtedly place ICE officers and contract guards at greater risk."[155] The union has also claimed that ICE initiated "this change in working conditions [referring to the detention reforms] without appropriate notice and an exercise of our bargaining rights... in violation of the current contract (Agreement 2000)."[156]

ICE field office directors—who serve as the managers of detention in 24 regions, or "field offices," throughout the country—have expressed concerns over any plans for what they call "an entirely 'soft' detention system," because, they argue, "there is a significant population with criminal convictions, arrest histories, gang affiliation,

psychological issues, drug abuse, etc., and these individuals pose a flight risk or security risk to ICE officers, other detainees and, at times, themselves." The field office directors assert that "[t]he structured environment that a more secure facility provides allows for greater command and control in a structured atmosphere, lending to greater security for both ICE officers, detainees, and the general public."[157]

However, not only is the kind of structured environment that exists in these jail-like immigration detention facilities unnecessarily costly and inappropriate for asylum seekers and other civil immigration law detainees,[158] but various experts on criminal prison systems have confirmed that "normalized environments" within secure facilities—rather than highly "structured" prison-like environments—can actually positively impact facility safety. For example, corrections expert Steve J. Martin, who worked as a prison guard, probation and parole officer, and prosecutor in the Texas prison system, and also served as the system's General Counsel, told Human Rights First in an interview that "the extent that you can normalize the confinement setting is the extent to which you can have a safe environment... For a population detained under civil authority, as long as I have the outside security envelope [i.e. perimeter fencing and/or a secure facility], everything within that envelope is maximized to whatever the budget and the institutional management might permit."[159] Furthermore, rather than a frivolous luxury, programming for detainees is considered a best practice in the corrections context; it helps fill detainees' time, which is otherwise mostly unoccupied, and thus contributes to a safer environment for detainees and officers alike.[160]

Moreover, DHS and ICE have indicated—since the first reform announcements—that while the government planned to develop more appropriate detention models for civil immigration law detainees, higher-risk detainees would be subject to some additional restrictions.[161] In its Statement of Objectives, ICE states:

> ICE recognizes that some detainees may have a criminal history. Consequently, detainees at the

medium and maximum classification levels may require housing in a more secure area of the facility. The new system will provide safe and secure conditions of confinement based on the individual characteristics of a diverse population, including: threat to the community, risk of flight, type and status of immigration proceeding, community ties, medical and mental health issues.[162]

Through an effective and automated risk classification assessment tool—which ICE has committed to implementing—ICE officers can identify individuals who may pose a danger and house them in facilities or areas of facilities that provide necessary protections for staff and other detainees, separate from lower-risk detainees. A standardized risk assessment tool is, however, a management tool – not a substitute for independent review of the need to detain. A risk classification assessment tool should identify detainee vulnerabilities as well as risk factors. Corrections experts have told Human Rights First in interviews that custody classifications (as well as release decisions) for detainees should be based on a range of factors, not just criminal history.[163]

Some ICE officers seem to be concerned that facilities designed for civil immigration law detainees would be designed in such a way that would permit immigration detainees to "walk away" from the facility. However, ICE has not proposed an end to the use of facilities with secure perimeters, but rather a shift in the conditions *within* the detention facilities. In fact, ICE has emphasized that it seeks to develop "supervised" facilities that are "safe and secure" and that "prevent unauthorized entry and egress."[164] The level of perimeter security necessary to prevent "walk-aways" must be distinguished from the

level of facility security necessary to ensure the safety of detainees and officers. As Michele Deitch, criminal justice and juvenile justice policy expert at the University of Texas, told Human Rights First in an interview: "A secure perimeter is for public safety purposes. Perimeter security should be distinguished from conditions inside a facility."[165]

ICE's plans to detain asylum seekers and other immigrants classified as "low risk" at its new facilities have raised concerns that ICE should not be expanding its capacity to detain individuals who could instead be released, whether through parole, bond, or an alternatives to detention program. In a February 2011 letter to DHS Secretary Napolitano, a group of Texas community, civil rights, and immigrant rights organizations urged that the administration "prioritize release of immigrants pending hearings, and the use of more humane, more effective, and more cost effective alternatives to detention programs," rather than building new immigration detention centers.[166] Many immigrant advocacy groups have expressed a range of other concerns about the construction of new facilities— including concerns about the continued escalation of immigration detention[167]; reports of assaults, abuses, and negligence leading to detainee deaths at facilities already run by the private prison companies that are slated to operate some of the new facilities[168]; and the lack of competitive bidding with respect to Delaney Hall in New Jersey.[169] On the other hand, local sheriff's departments that depend on ICE funding to provide jobs to the community may resist the U.S. government's attempts to close jails that are inappropriate to hold ICE detainees. This has already occurred in Alabama, where resistance from local elected officials actually prevented ICE from ending its contract with the Etowah jail.[170]

Progress to Improve Existing Detention System

In 2009, DHS not only committed to making a shift to non-penal detention conditions for ICE detainees, but also to make improvements to the immigration detention system more broadly. These commitments followed years of reports—by governmental bodies, non-governmental organizations, and the media—documenting serious problems in the detention system, including inadequate medical and mental health treatment, detainee deaths in custody, excessive transfers undermining access to legal counsel and families, and noncompliance with existing standards.[171] ICE's reform announcements promised "improved medical care, custodial conditions, fiscal prudence, and ICE oversight" in the immigration detention system.[172]

Over the past two years, ICE has taken a number of significant steps toward improving the existing detention system.[173] The agency has centralized management of all contracts in a single office and reduced the number of facilities from 341 to 254. It launched an online detainee locator that allows family and legal counsel to find out where an individual is being held, and created a new internal policy to systematize reporting of detainee deaths in ICE custody. It also streamlined the process for detainee health care treatment authorizations and modified the medical benefits package for ICE detainees to provide for treatment for serious, non-emergency medical needs.[174]

ICE also developed a risk classification assessment tool for its officers to use to systematize detainee release and/or custody classification decisions and improve oversight of these decisions, addressing a major management gap in the detention system. It revised its parole guidance so that detained asylum seekers who pass credible fear screening interviews after arrival are automatically assessed for potential parole eligibility. ICE statistics show that this new guidance has significantly increased the number of asylum seekers assessed for parole, and that the release rate under the new guidance has remained within 9 percent of the release rate in 2009, prior to the new guidance. [175]This new guidance

will need to be codified into regulations to ensure lasting change.

The agency has hired and trained 42 detention service managers to provide full-time onsite monitoring of the largest immigration detention facilities, and these monitors report back to headquarters in Washington. It has developed an access policy to permit nongovernmental organization representatives to tour detention facilities and speak with detainees more easily, and a detainee transfer policy that, when implemented, is intended to systematize transfer practices. ICE has also taken steps it says will reduce detainee transfers– by geographically re-aligning detention "capacity" and detention "need" (though ICE has not publicly committed to closing existing facilities as it makes plans to open new ones). The ICE Office of Detention Policy and Planning— created to direct the reform efforts—has also improved transparency and communication, regularly meeting with nongovernmental organizations that work with detained asylum seekers and other immigrants, as well as with other stakeholders in the detention system.

Finally, in June 2011, ICE issued new guidance on the use of prosecutorial discretion by ICE personnel,[176] which may impact detention and release decisions. In August 2011, the Administration also announced plans to review 300,000 cases in removal proceedings, including detained cases, and administratively close the cases of low-priority individuals, which has the potential to reduce the backlog of cases in immigration courts and improve case processing times.[177] These last two new policies may change the composition of the detained population—though they do not change the need for reform of conditions.

These are all important and welcome improvements to policy and practice that should exist for any system that detains or incarcerates people, whether correctional or civil in nature.

Persistent Deficiencies

"The last day before my release, they brought me back to the immigration office in Virginia, and I was dragged to the asylum officer's room for credible fear interview. My legs were tied and my hands were tied, and I said, Oh my god, how big a crime did I do? They treated me as if I was a criminal, and I had not committed any crime."

–Nepalese asylum seeker detained in 2011 in an immigration detention facility in Virginia

Despite these steps forward, published reports of deficiencies in the immigration detention system have persisted over the past two years—including, in recent months, severe noncompliance with detention standards at Pinal County jail in Arizona (423 detainees),[178] problems with legal access, conditions, and medical and mental health care at Otero County Processing Center in New Mexico (746 detainees),[179] and improper use of segregation for LGBT detainees throughout the immigration detention system.[180] The December 2010 Inter-American Commission on Human Rights report on U.S. detention practices flagged, among other issues, ongoing concerns relating to detainee medical and mental health care, including insufficient covered services of medical and dental care, chronic and severe staffing shortages among medical and mental health personnel across the system, and inappropriate use of administrative segregation (i.e. solitary confinement) for mentally ill detainees.[181]

In March 2011, the DHS Office of the Inspector General released a report that identified a number of problems in the delivery of mental health services to ICE detainees, including inadequate oversight, insufficient staffing, facility designs and locations that hinder mental health care for detainees, and unclear decision-making authorities for transfer of detainees with mental health care needs.[182]

Over the past two years, the Departments of Justice and Homeland Security have declined to accept the recommendations of the bipartisan federal National Prison Rape Elimination Commission relating to standards for facilities holding immigration detainees.

Hutto Detention Center in Taylor, Texas, holds 450 ICE detainees.

The Commission was created by Congress to propose standards to "prevent, detect, respond to and monitor sexual abuse of incarcerated or detained individuals throughout the United States." In its final report, in June 2009, it found that "[a] large and growing number of detained immigrants are at risk of sexual abuse. Their heightened vulnerability and unusual circumstances require special interventions."[183] The Commission developed supplemental standards to apply to any facility holding immigration detainees, but these standards have yet to be adopted by DHS. Instead, DHS incorporated less detailed sexual abuse standards into the draft 2010 PBNDS. Earlier this year, the Department of Justice proposed standards under the Prison Rape Elimination Act of 2003 (PREA) that exclude from PREA coverage facilities holding primarily immigration detainees."[184]

Unnecessary Costs from Unnecessary Detention: Lack of Fair and Effective Release Procedures

The U.S. immigration detention system lacks some basic safeguards, rendering it inconsistent with U.S. concepts of fairness and international human rights standards. For example, the initial decision to detain an asylum seeker who requests protection at a U.S. airport or border is "mandatory" under the expedited removal provisions of the 1996 immigration laws. The decision to release an asylum seeker on parole—or to continue his or her detention for longer—is entrusted to local officials with ICE, which is the detaining authority, rather than to an independent authority or at least an immigration court.[185] Several other categories of immigrants are also subjected to "mandatory" detention, and are also deprived of access to immigration court custody hearings.[186] While U.S. immigration authorities have expanded their use of Alternatives to Detention in recent years, the government still does not have nationwide capacity to use Alternatives to Detention, despite the substantial cost-savings of these programs.

Lack of Immigration Court Custody Review for Arriving Asylum Seekers and Others

Asylum seekers who request protection at U.S. airports and borders are precluded under regulatory language from requesting review of their detention from an immigration judge[187]—making their detention arbitrary under international human rights law.[188] ICE acts, in effect, as both judge and jailor with respect to parole decisions for these asylum seekers. If parole is denied, the decision cannot be appealed to a judge—even an immigration judge.[189]

Although ICE issued revised parole guidance for asylum seekers, which went into effect in January 2010, that guidance is not in regulations, and in any event, is not a substitute for prompt independent court review. (The prior parole guidance, from November 2007, had been criticized by Human Rights First and other groups, including the U.S. Commission on International Religious Freedom, which was concerned that the guidance was

inconsistent with recommendations it made in its 2005 report on U.S. detention of asylum seekers.)

In March 2010, the National Immigrant Justice Center and other U.S. nongovernmental organizations filed petitions for rulemaking with the Departments of Homeland Security and Justice requesting that they promulgate parole regulations and provide access to immigration court custody reviews for arriving asylum seekers who pass initial credible fear screening interviews.[190] In 2010, in the course of the Universal Periodic Review conducted by the U.N. Human Rights Council of U.S. compliance with its international human rights obligations, Human Rights First and many other groups also urged that the U.S. government provide arriving asylum seekers and other immigrants with the chance to have their custody reviewed before an immigration court.[191] In December 2010, the Department of Homeland Security advised that it did not intend to propose parole regulations, and did not intend to provide for release of arriving asylum seekers through immigration court custody hearings.[192] The petition for rulemaking is still under consideration at the Department of Justice.

In the course of the Universal Periodic Review, many U.S. civil society groups also recommended that U.S. laws be reformed to allow other categories of immigrants—who are denied access to immigration court custody hearings under "mandatory detention" provisions in a 1996 immigration law—to have access to immigration court custody hearings.[193]

Alternatives to Detention

A number of supervised-release programs, known as "alternatives to detention," have been successfully tested in the United States. These programs have been repeatedly demonstrated to lead to substantial cost-savings and high compliance rates in the United States, and also around the world. Alternatives to Detention programs provide for release from immigration detention with some additional measures to monitor an individual after release. These measures can include in-person reporting, telephonic reporting, and home visits. Some programs also use electronic ankle monitors, though significant restrictions on movement can rise to the level of custody, as described below.

In its October 2009 reform announcements, ICE highlighted the cost-effectiveness of Alternatives to Detention. In April 2010, it submitted a report to Congress describing several scenarios for nationwide expansion of ATDs, which stated that Alternatives to Detention cost ICE on average $8.88 per day [194] – more than $110 less per day than detention.[195] ICE has not requested—and Congress has yet to authorize—sufficient funding to expand ATD programs nationally—so that any immigration detainee who is eligible for an ATD program could be placed into it, leading to substantial governmental savings as well as more appropriate environments for individual immigration detainees.

Alternatives to Detention are currently provided to ICE under a new consolidated contract with BI Incorporated, a private company owned by the publicly traded prison contractor GEO Group. ICE places Alternatives to Detention enrollees into one of two programs—a "full-service" program and a "technology-only" program. The full-service program provides enrollees with "intensive case management, supervision, electronic monitoring, and individuals service plans." The technology-only program uses GPS tracking and phone reporting. BI says that they help "mitigate flight risk and guide the participant through the immigration court process." In a forthcoming report, Lutheran Immigration and Refugee Service, a nonprofit organization that has piloted ATD programs in the past, has found that the case management services provided by BI are inadequate to their purpose.[196] Still, according to BI's annual report to the U.S. government, in 2010, 93 percent of individuals actively enrolled in ATDs attended their final court hearings, and 84 percent complied with removal orders.[197]

As noted above, ICE's annual detention budget exceeds $2 billion, with an average cost of $122 per day per immigration detainee. ICE's April 2010 report

U.S. HUMAN RIGHTS COMMITMENTS
Prompt Court Review And Alternatives To Detention

The United States has committed to comply with the provisions of various international human rights conventions, including the Refugee Convention, its 1967 Protocol, and the International Covenant on Civil and Political Rights (ICCPR).[198] Consistent with these commitments, the United States should only detain after a consideration of alternative measures to detention, and when asylum seekers or migrants are detained, they should be provided with prompt and independent court review.

As detailed by UNHCR in a comprehensive legal study published in April 2011, detention should only be used as a last resort after considering alternative measures to detention.[199] In order to establish that detention is necessary, and not arbitrary within the meaning of the ICCPR, States must consider the "less invasive means of achieving the same ends."[200]

Article 9(4) of the ICCPR provides that "Anyone who is deprived of his liberty by arrest or detention shall be entitled to take proceedings *before a court*, in order that the court may decide without delay on the lawfulness of his detention and order his release if the detention is not lawful."[201] The review must be provided by a court in order to ensure objectivity and independence,[202] and must also be effective, not just pro forma, providing a real inquiry into the necessity of detention.[203] Guidelines issued by the U.N. High Commissioner for Refugees similarly call for "automatic review before a judicial or administrative body independent of the detaining authority" when detention is used.[204]

Both the U.N. Special Rapporteur on the Human Rights of Migrants and the Inter-American Commission on Human Rights have concluded that the U.S. detention system lacks safeguards and measures required under international human rights law and standards, and they have recommended that the United States ensure that the decision to detain a non-citizen is promptly assessed by an independent court and that immigration courts be allowed to review release decisions made by immigration officers.[205]

Even with more appropriate detention conditions, detention can still be—and is—penal in nature when it runs afoul of other human rights protection—for example, when detention is not necessary, reasonable, or proportionate, or is unnecessarily prolonged.[206]

estimates that it will cost $88 million, at a minimum, to expand ATD programs nationwide, and more likely somewhere between $88 million and $513 million—depending on the average length of time that an individual remains in an ATD program and the total number of individuals enrolled in ATDs.[207] The plan outlines a scenario, however, that would *not* use ATDs as an alternative that would decrease the use of existing detention beds—thereby saving money—but would instead use these programs to increase ICE's apprehension and detention of immigrants with criminal histories subject to mandatory detention (primarily through an enforcement program called Secure Communities), displacing from detention those immigration detainees who are not subject to mandatory detention. According to its plan, ICE would enroll individuals not subject to mandatory detention in ATD programs, and its detention facilities would be occupied entirely by immigrants subject to mandatory detention. The total number of individuals in ICE custody or supervision, whether detained or on Alternatives to Detention, would increase under this plan.

ICE's plan also explicitly precludes the use of ATDs for individuals who are technically subject to "mandatory detention," though a formal recognition that the use of restrictive forms of monitoring can amount to custody could pave the way for the use of ATDs in some of these cases as well (where appropriate based on an individualized assessment).[208] The approach reflected in the April 2010 report appears to be consistent with plans by officials in the prior administration[209] to use ATDs to expand the number of individuals subject to detention or supervision, rather than to use ATDs to reduce overall detention costs by releasing individuals who do not require a costly stay in detention in order to meet the government's objectives.

The ATD program remains a small proportion of ICE's total budget for detention and removal. ICE's requested budget for detention in fiscal year 2012 was $2.02 billion—28 times its requested budget of $72.4 million for Alternatives to Detention.[210]

Several successful ATD programs have been piloted in the United States over the years, including programs run by the Vera Institute of Justice and by Lutheran Immigration and Refugee Service. These programs documented high appearance rates, and saved government funds by allowing for the release of individuals from more costly immigration detention.[211] According to multiple studies, successful Alternatives to Detention programs, in the United States and around the world, typically include the following components: individualized case assessment, individualized case management including referrals, legal advice, access to adequate accommodations, information about rights and duties and consequences of non-compliance, and humane and respectful treatment.[212]

Cost of Detention Versus Cost of Alternatives to Detention (ATDs)[213]

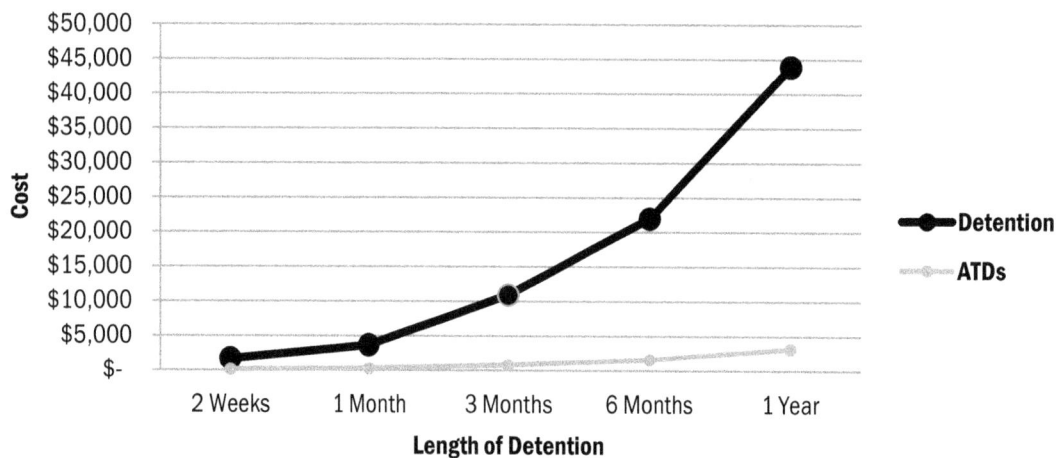

Risk Classification Assessment Tool

In October 2011, in response to an inquiry on the status of development of a risk classification assessment tool, senior ICE officials advised Human Rights First that:

> ICE has devised and is now beginning to implement a new detainee intake process to improve the consistency and transparency of ICE's custody and release decisions. The risk assessment tool contains objective criteria to guide decision-making regarding whether or not an alien should be detained or released; the alien's custody classification level, if detained; and the alien's level of community supervision (to include an ICE ATD program), if released. Using the tool, immigration officers will be more likely to identify any special vulnerabilities that may affect custody determinations. In fact, the risk assessment tool includes the following special vulnerabilities that many NGOs on the Director's Advisory Group for Detention had recommended be taken into consideration: disability, advanced age, pregnancy, nursing mothers, sole caretaking responsibilities, mental health issues, or victimization, including aliens who may be eligible for relief related under the Violence Against Women Act (VAWA), victims of crime (U visa), or victims of human trafficking (T visa).

> ICE has also developed training for our officers to identify vulnerable populations and has consulted with the DHS' Office for Civil Rights and Civil Liberties (CRCL) and NGOs on special training topics. In addition, CRCL has provided specialized training to a corps of new detention managers that included civil rights considerations in the treatment of asylum seekers and recognizing victims of trafficking. The training also covered the special needs of women in detention and mental health issues that our facilities are often called upon to address.

> The Risk Assessment is now being automated in ENFORCE. The automation effort is proceeding well and will ensure that the Risk Assessment Tool is institutionalized. The target date for completion of the automation and training of officers is January 2012.[214]

This type of systematic assessment was recommended by Dr. Schriro in the 2009 DHS-ICE report,[215] and the need for it was also emphasized in a 2009 report issued by the Migration Policy Institute. A standardized risk assessment is a management tool—not a substitute for independent review of the need to detain – and one of many necessary steps that can assist in allowing for significant cost-savings by shifting some individuals from detention to Alternatives to Detention or release on bond. Dr. James Austin, one of the nation's foremost experts on custody classification in the criminal context, has explained that classification tools help determine when a prisoner should be released and under what forms of supervision and services.[216]

If the data used during risk assessment is linked appropriately to a centralized database through this new tool, the tool may provide much-needed information about release processes and classification decisions at all facilities in the detention system, improving the potential for oversight and accountability. ICE still needs to develop triggers for re-running the assessment, so that, for example, asylum seekers who have passed their credible fear screening interviews and are thus no longer subject to mandatory detention will automatically be re-assessed for release. The agency also needs to set aside sufficient resources to evaluate the tool through a validation process after it has been fully implemented, to ensure that it is leading to appropriate individual outcomes, and to revise scoring or other aspects of the tool if it is not.

Inadequate Access to Legal Assistance and Justice, Particularly in Isolated Detention Facilities

As detailed in Human Rights First's 2009 report, as DHS and ICE expanded immigration detention, they repeatedly chose to detain asylum seekers and other immigrants in facilities located in areas that are not near pro bono legal resources, the immigration courts, or U.S. asylum offices.[217] Detained asylum seekers and other detained immigrants have very little access to legal representation or even legal information, and the location of many immigration detention facilities can add to the already significant difficulty of finding and retaining competent counsel. At many of these remote facilities, immigration officials are also—increasingly—turning to the use of video-conferencing to conduct immigration court hearings and even credible fear screening interviews, compounding the challenges that immigration detainees face in accessing justice.

Krome North Service Processing Center in Miami holds 600 ICE detainees.

Legal Representation and Legal Orientation Programs

The overwhelming majority of asylum seekers and immigrants who are held in immigration detention—84 percent—are not represented by legal counsel in removal proceedings, in which they defend themselves against the government's efforts to deport them. Only 16 percent of detained immigrants are represented by legal counsel in these proceedings.[218] The U.S. government does not provide funding for legal representation for asylum seekers and other immigrants in their asylum and immigration proceedings. Yet the importance of counsel cannot be overstated.

U.S. immigration law is a complex mix of laws that derive from the Immigration and Nationality Act (INA) and the

implementing regulations detailed in the Code of Federal Regulations, and are also governed by a combination of decisions issued by the U.S. Supreme Court, 13 different Federal Circuit Courts, the Board of Immigration Appeals, and various memos issued by multiple federal agencies, including the Departments of State, Justice, and Homeland Security. Immigration law is further complicated by the intersection of the INA and the thousands of federal and state criminal statutes that may or may not trigger a ground of inadmissibility or removability—mandatory or discretionary—or a ground of mandatory detention. Moreover, an immigrant's eligibility for relief from removal often hinges on such particular factual details that formulating legal arguments in favor of or against relief requires a sophisticated understanding of all the relevant statutes, regulations, case law, and agency memos as applied in individual circumstances.

For asylum seekers, several studies have documented the impact of legal representation on success rates, including a study by the Government Accountability Office, which found "more than a three-fold increase" in the asylum grant rate for asylum seekers who were represented, as compared to those without representation.[219] More broadly, the Department of Justice's Executive Office for Immigration Review (EOIR) has expressed "great concern" about the large number of individuals appearing in immigration court without representation, and has also noted that "[n]on-represented cases are more difficult to conduct," and that they require additional effort and time from immigration judges.[220] Immigration proceedings are a daunting labyrinth for any individual to navigate alone—especially as the consequence of deportation is tremendous—yet the majority of detained immigrants go through the process not only without counsel, but also without sufficient opportunity to seek counsel or access legal information.

While not a substitute for legal representation, the highly successful Legal Orientation Program (LOP)—an EOIR program managed through a contract with the Vera Institute for Justice, which subcontracts with local non-profit legal service providers—offers basic legal information to immigrant detainees so that they can understand their legal options, and helps connect them to pro bono resources. [221] LOP has received widespread praise for promoting the efficiency and effectiveness of the removal process, and immigration judges have lauded LOP for better preparing immigrants to identify forms of relief.[222] Although the President's fiscal year 2012 budget request recognized the success of LOP and sought to expand its reach by almost doubling the program's funding over FY 2011 levels, Congress has not provided appropriations accordingly.[223] EOIR is funded to operate the LOP in just 25 detention facilities, reaching only approximately 15 percent of detained immigrants and 35 percent of detained immigrants in EOIR proceedings annually.

Geographic Isolation

The remote locations of many immigration detention facilities increase the difficulty of securing legal representation for asylum seekers and other immigration detainees. In its 2005 study on asylum seekers in expedited removal, the bipartisan U.S. Commission on International Religious Freedom found that many of the facilities used to detain asylum seekers were "located in rural parts of the United States, where few lawyers visit and even fewer maintain a practice." The Commission concluded that "[t]he practical effect of detention in remote locations...is to restrict asylum seekers' legally authorized right to counsel."[224] In a 2009 survey, the National Immigrant Justice Center found that "80 percent of detainees were held in facilities which were severely underserved by legal aid organizations, with more than 100 detainees for every full-time NGO attorney providing legal services. More than a quarter of detainees were in facilities that were even more grossly underserved, where the ratio was 500 or more detainees per NGO attorney. A full 10 percent of detainees were held in facilities in which they had no access to NGO attorneys whatsoever."[225]

According to Human Rights First calculations, almost 40 percent of ICE's total bed space is located more than 60 miles from an urban center.[226] Among these, ICE detains immigrants at several facilities that are particularly remote, including:

- Jena/LaSalle Detention Center (220 miles from New Orleans, 138 miles from Baton Rouge)—1,106 ICE beds

- South Louisiana Detention Center (170 mil from New Orleans, 92 miles from Baton Rouge)—391 ICE beds

- Tensas Parish Detention Center (201 miles from New Orleans, 122 miles from Baton Rouge)—134 ICE beds

- Utah County Jail (53 miles from Salt Lake City, 475 miles from Denver)—200 ICE beds

- West Texas Detention Facility (400 miles from Tucson)—153 ICE beds

- Port Isabel (155 miles from Corpus Christi)—857 ICE beds

- Irwin County Detention Center (180 miles from Atlanta, 100 miles from Tallahassee)—295 ICE beds

Remote locations not only undermine access to legal counsel, but they can also affect the staffing of the medical and mental health services at a facility by limiting access to a pool of qualified medical professionals.[227] In addition, the location of some of these facilities—far from detainees' families and sometimes far from public transportation—can make family visits difficult to impossible.

Video-Conference Hearings

As detailed in Human Rights First's 2009 report, increasingly, immigrant detainees are seen by judges in the course of their removal proceedings only via video-conference—i.e., on a television screen in a courtroom or other room in the detention facility. Likewise, some detainees seeking asylum receive their screening interviews—known as credible fear interviews—via video-conference. Of the 17 facilities visited by Human Rights First in 2010 and 2011, EOIR uses video-conference capabilities to conduct immigration court hearings for detainees in at least 10 of them: James A. Musick, Port Isabel, Broward Transitional Center, Glades County (for the female detainees; men are transported to Krome for their hearings), ICA-Farmville, Hutto, Pearsall, Berks, Willacy, and Hudson County (for cases at the Newark immigration court; detainees with cases in New York are transported to the New York immigration court at Varick Street). The DHS-USCIS Asylum Office uses video-conferencing or telephone to conduct credible fear and reasonable fear interviews for detainees in at least three of the facilities: Pearsall, Berks, and Hutto.

Human Rights First has identified a range of concerns regarding the increasing use of video-conferencing for removal hearings and credible fear interviews. These concerns include the difficulty of testifying to torture and traumatic events and the challenges of assessing credibility through video-conference testimony, as well as the problem that a federal court has called a "Catch-22" choice—requiring an attorney to decide between the ability to confer with a client during a hearing and the opportunity to "interact effectively" with the judge and opposing counsel.[228] In 2010, the Inter-American Commission on Human Rights, in its comprehensive report on the U.S. immigration detention system, stressed that it was "deeply concerned with the increasing reliance on video conferencing for immigration proceedings."[229] The combination of isolated facilities—along with the inadequate funding for the immigration courts, and the proportionally much greater funding for immigration enforcement efforts that are increasing the case load of the immigration courts—may lead to a further increase in the use of video-conferencing.

Moving Forward: Key Conditions in a "Civil" Immigration Detention System

As detailed above, the vast majority of immigration detainees continue to be held in jails or jail-like facilities in penal conditions. At the same time, DHS and ICE leadership have repeatedly voiced a commitment to transform the system by reducing reliance on penal facilities. In their 2010 Statement of Objectives (SOO), DHS and ICE again confirmed this commitment by stressing that "[a] key goal of Immigration Detention Reform is to create a civil detention system that is not penal in nature."[230] ICE already holds detainees in a few facilities with some less penal conditions—including Broward Transitional Center, Hutto Detention Center, and Berks Family Detention Center. The agency has developed several additional facilities that it says will reflect conditions that are more appropriate for civil immigration law detainees. The SOO—the only public ICE document that describes the agency's vision for civil detention—is reproduced in the appendix to this report. It calls for conditions including:

■ Enhanced but controlled freedom of movement

■ Cafeteria-style meals

■ Indoor and outdoor community areas with non-institutional furniture

■ Extended outdoor recreation hours in a space that allows for aerobic exercise

■ Contact visitation

■ Private attorney-client meeting areas

■ Programming

■ Fully staffed medical and mental health facilities

■ Natural light

■ "Non-traditional" detention uniforms/clothing

■ Qualified and trained staff.

Some of these conditions are less restrictive and more "normalized" than the conditions that currently exist in the majority of ICE-authorized detention facilities. Though

ICE and DHS have called these conditions "non-penal," many of them actually do exist in the corrections context as well—or should exist in any facility that detains or incarcerates—and are touted as best practices to improve facility safety and humane treatment for many prison populations. In fact, the American Bar Association's 2010 Criminal Justice Standards on Treatment of Prisoners, which represent best practices, call for many of these same elements—including contact visits, some privacy, and expanded outdoor recreation—in both correctional and immigration detention facilities.[231] Immigration detention facilities should not be modeled on correctional facilities, but they should certainly not be operated with *more* restrictions than corrections experts believe correctional facilities should have.

The impact of prison design and operations on safety has been the subject of many studies,[232] particularly as prison and jail designs began to shift toward direct-supervision models (away from a traditional "corridor" design) in the late 1960s and early 1970s with the goal of creating safer and more humane environments for inmates and officers. A central component (among others) of these direct-supervision models was "a normalized living environment, meaning that the interior of the facilities would have a less institutional feel to it."[233] Maximizing the choice and autonomy available to inmates was also important in the direct-supervision model.[234] Multiple experts have argued that normalized conditions—such as some degree of free movement within the facility, some privacy, natural light, comfortable and non-institutional furniture, tile or carpet flooring, and porcelain toilets (rather than stainless steel)—can contribute to improved safety inside a facility. These conditions can also provide a disincentive to inmate misbehavior, since misbehavior could be punished with a move to less desirable housing.

By way of explanation, the former warden of the Chicago Metropolitan Correctional Center, which was one of the first direct-supervision models, wrote, "[I]n essence, an environment designed to be indestructible evokes destructive behavior, while an environment designed for normal usage evokes normal behavior."[238] Reviewing a number of studies conducted in the course of two decades on direct-supervision jails with "normalized" environments, one researcher concluded: "This is not to say that the jail will be converted into a luxurious setting, but if architects and administrators work to develop a normalized physical and social environment, the potential for reduction of inmate and officer stress, violence, and property damage exists."[239]

Prison wardens, corrections experts, and long-time corrections professionals interviewed by Human Rights First confirmed these observations linking normalized environments in detention to improved safety within a facility. Steve J. Martin, who worked as a prison guard, prosecutor, and former General Counsel in the Texas prison system, said, "The extent that you can normalize the confinement setting is the extent to which you can have a safe environment... For a population detained under civil authority, as long as I have the outside security envelope [i.e. perimeter fencing and/or a secure facility], everything within that envelope is maximized to whatever the budget and the institutional management might permit.... To the extent that we're imposing these

limitations, we're criminalizing their civil status." Martin described the essential elements of a more normalized environment: maximum freedom of movement within the physical plant, outdoor space with dedicated area for sports or other activities (not just an empty yard inside a fence), privacy in toilets and showers, Internet access, common day space for congregate activity, and programming. He added, "Within reasonable limitations, there's no reason not to permit civilian clothing."[240]

A normalized detention environment can positively impact prison facilities holding higher-risk detainees as well as low-risk detainees.[241] For example, McKean Federal Correctional Institution, a medium-security federal prison, was praised in the mid-1990s as "the best-managed prison in the country." It housed more than 1,000 men, saw much less violence than was typical, and was significantly less expensive per inmate than the system-wide average. McKean offered "open" movement throughout the facility, generous recreation time, and a pleasant and comfortable physical environment." The long-time warden, Dennis Luther, reported:

> On a summer evening you've got three to five hundred men in this rec yard, with three staff. If you had less recreation, you'd need more staff. There's a clear economic advantage. You'd *definitely* have more fights. We do surveys every year, and they show that as inmates get more involved in the rec program, they get in less trouble. Also, they tend to have less health trouble, and that saves money.

Luther "insists that physical details [such as carpets, sofas, and plants] help to maintain order, just as the programs do." One of Luther's primary principles: "Normalize the environment to the extent possible by providing programs, amenities, and services. The denial of such must be related to maintaining order and security rather than punishment. Most inmates will respond favorably to a clean and aesthetically pleasing physical environment and will not vandalize or destroy it."[242]

Medical experts have found that an immigration detainee's lack of control over details of his living environment—"from the clothes he wears; to the number of hours he sleeps; to the degree of light or darkness in his cell; to the food he eats; to the sounds he hears; to the amount and quality of the fresh air he breathes; to the degree of physical activity or inactivity in which he engages; and the people with whom he communicates"—can exacerbate stress.[243] Bolstering the corrections professionals' recommendations that normalized detention environments promote safe facilities, such medical assessments suggest that a normalized environment can also be beneficial to the mental health of immigrant detainees.

In 2008 recommendations to the incoming Obama administration and in a 2009 report on the detention of asylum seekers in the United States, Human Rights First recommended that immigration detention facilities holding asylum seekers and other civil immigration detainees should permit detainees to wear their own clothing, have real outdoor access, have freedom of movement within a secure facility, and have contact visits.

Human Rights First continues to urge ICE—over the next two years—to prioritize its commitment to move the U.S. immigration detention system away from its reliance on jails and jail-like facilities. Instead, all facilities holding ICE detainees should include a range of conditions, programming, and other measures more appropriate for immigration law detainees. Some of the conditions that should exist in all immigration detention facilities—and that should be detailed in the standards that govern them—include:

1) Increased freedom of movement within a secure facility.

Using a proven custody classification tool appropriate to the ICE civil detainee population, as well as modern technology, ICE should provide detained asylum seekers and other immigration law detainees with the ability to move freely within a secure facility and its grounds, among their housing unit, outdoor recreation area, indoor recreation or common space, library, cafeteria, and any other program or support area. Rather than multiple daily head counts, which disrupt the day by requiring detainees to remain in their housing units for up to an hour at a time, ICE could use a check-in system modeled on the system already in use at Hutto Detention Facility.

At most of the 254 ICE-authorized detention facilities, immigrant detainees are confined to their pod or cell for up to 23 hours per day. They typically cannot leave their housing units to access outdoor recreation, indoor recreation, the library, or the cafeteria except during limited periods of time, and then only with an escort, even though the facility grounds are surrounded by perimeter fencing and the buildings themselves are also secure. They are subject to multiple daily head counts, which disrupt the day by requiring detainees to remain in their housing units for up to an hour at a time. The 2009 DHS-ICE report noted, "Movement is largely restricted and detainees spend the majority of their time in their housing units.... Access to recreation, religious services, the law library, and visitation can be improved."[244]

Former prison officials and corrections experts recommend that freedom of movement be maximized within a secure facility, taking into account propensity to violence suggested by prior behavior in an institutional setting. They emphasize that technology such as security cameras should be used to ensure safety and permit the greatest level of freedom of movement to detainees. For example, Jeanne Woodford, former warden of San Quentin State Prison and former Acting Secretary of the California Department of Corrections, explained in an interview with a Human Rights First researcher that "the degree of freedom of movement granted to inmates should be as much as possible, based on behavior."[245] Former General Counsel to the Texas prison system Steve J. Martin similarly told Human Rights First that "freedom of movement should be maximized within the restrictions of the physical plant. Detainees should have fairly free access to move from point A to point B. Fixed cameras can be used to monitor detainees."[246] And Martin Horn, who ran the corrections systems in Pennsylvania and New York City, said, "Most immigration detainees without criminal history could be moving freely... Inmates with no prior violations of security, no assaults, and no enemies can and should move freely observed by cameras and intermittent check stops staffed by security staff."[247]

Four existing ICE-authorized facilities already permit greater movement for detainees within their secure grounds. The strategies used for providing increased movement at these facilities could serve as models for the rest of the immigration detention system.

Berks Family Detention Center (Pennsylvania): Berks has permitted freedom of movement to male and female detainees, as well as their children, for more than two years. Detainees are not locked into their rooms, and may walk throughout the facility and the grounds without restriction from 6am to 8pm every day. The main building itself is secure, but the grounds are not surrounded by a perimeter fence. From 8pm to 6am, detainees must remain in their housing wings, which include a common area with a television and comfortable chairs. According to a county staff member interviewed by Human Rights First, the facility's staff were initially "skeptical" about the practicability of increased movement in the facility, but now they "cannot imagine it otherwise." The staff person, who reported that he was initially skeptical himself, now said, "I am a big fan of free movement."[248] After a visit to Berks, Vincent Cochetel, the U.N. refugee agency's regional representative for the United States, recommended that the facility serve as a best practice model, rather than the exception, for the immigration detention system. In a January 2011 statement, Cochetel stressed that "[i]n the rare event that it is determined that an asylum-seeker should be detained, then the Berks facility embodies many of the best practices for a truly civil immigration detention model... .We encourage ICE to make Berks the standard—not the exception—for its network of detention facilities across the country."[249]

Broward Transitional Center (Florida): The dormitories at Broward Transitional Center are constructed on two levels around a large courtyard, which serves as outdoor recreation space. The men's dorm rooms, which house up to six men apiece, open into the courtyard or the balcony overlooking the courtyard on the second floor. The library/law library and two rooms for religious observance are located among the men's rooms. The women's housing area consists of a long hallway of dorm rooms, which house up to six women apiece, plus an indoor recreation room. They are free to move throughout this area for most of the day. The men are permitted to move freely outdoors and indoors from 6am until dark, except for four hours each day, when their movement is restricted to half the courtyard so that the female detainees can access outdoor recreation and/or the library/law library. This inequity was one of several concerns Human Rights First had with the facility during our visit.[250] The layout itself does, however, facilitate improved freedom of movement among detainees.

T. Don Hutto Residential Center (Texas): Though Hutto was designed as a prison, it held immigrant families until September 2009, when ICE converted it to a women-only facility.[251] Reforms made following the settlement of a major lawsuit against ICE in 2007[252] have meant that detainees can now move freely among dormitory rooms, common areas, and outdoor recreation areas from 8am to 8pm every day. The facility is secure—meaning

detainees are prevented from leaving—but in accordance with family residential standards, doors inside the facility do not lock. An assistant field office director informed Human Rights First that freedom of movement has not caused any problems at Hutto. The facility's medical staff also said that freedom of movement allows detainees easier access to medical care.[253]

Immigration Centers of America-Farmville (Virginia): ICA was designed as a prison, but opened as an ICE-only facility in August 2010. During a tour in September 2010, Human Rights First was told that immigration detainees are permitted to move throughout the facility 24 hours a day. So, for instance, detainees can leave their housing units (large dormitories with pinwheel bunks) to go to the outdoor recreation area or the library at any hour (though they eat their meals in their housing units; there is no cafeteria). The facility uses technology to monitor detainee movement. Each detainee wears a scannable wristband at all times, using it to check in to any destination within the facility. He must inform staff of his destination, and if too much time elapses before he checks in to that destination, a staff member is sent out to locate him.[254]

Aside from these four facilities, ICE-authorized detention centers permit only very limited movement to detainees. More significant freedom of movement is actually permitted, to varying degrees, in federal correctional facilities across the country. These facilities include:

- All 6 Federal Bureau of Prisons minimum-security institutions, known as Federal Prison Camps (FPCs)—including Alderson (West Virginia), Bryan (Texas), Duluth (Minnesota), Montgomery (Alabama), Pensacola (Florida), and Yankton (South Dakota)

- All 29 Federal Bureau of Prisons low-security institutions, known as low-security Federal Correctional Institutions (FCIs)—including Allenwood Low (Pennsylvania), Bastrop (Texas), Beaumont Low (Texas), Coleman Low (Florida), Danbury (Connecticut), Englewood (Colorado), Lompoc (California), Oakdale (Louisiana), Petersburg Low (Virginia), Safford (Arizona), and Texarkana (Texas).[255]

In each of these facilities, which together house over 80,000 federal prisoners,[256] inmates can generally exit and enter their housing area without an escort, walking to and from their job sites, the cafeteria, the indoor and outdoor recreation areas, the visitation room, the doctor, and the library.

Corrections facilities should not serve as models for the immigration detention system. However, the facts that many federal Bureau of Prisons facilities allow greater freedom of movement than most immigration detention facilities, and that prison experts confirm the need for maximum freedom of movement, strongly suggest that most civil immigration law detainees should be permitted greater mobility within secure facilities than they presently receive.

2) Non-prison clothing for detainees

Individuals who are detained for administrative purposes under the immigration law should be allowed to wear their own clothing, or at the very least civilian clothing that does not resemble uniforms.

At all but two of the 254 ICE-authorized detention facilities, immigration detainees—who are not being held on criminal charges—wear prison uniforms or prison jumpsuits. These uniforms are typically color-coded according to the detainees' custody classifications, though sometimes they are simply whatever color the facility has on hand. Current ICE detention standards mandate the color-coded uniforms—dark blue for low-risk, bright orange for medium-risk, and dark red for high-risk.[257] However, ICE's family residential detention standards actually permit detainees to wear their own clothing and mandate that the facility provide to those who need it clothing that "shall not resemble institutional-style clothing."[258]

Hutto Residential Center and Berks Family Residential Center are the only two ICE-authorized facilities that permit detainees to wear their own clothing, or clothing donated by the community. (They are both inspected against ICE's family residential standards.) When Human Rights First researchers visited these facilities, we observed men, women, and children wearing jeans, t-shirts, blouses, sweatshirts, and other regular clothes. As a result, not only do these detained asylum seekers and other immigrants live—during the weeks and months that they are held in immigration detention—in civilian clothing rather than prison uniforms, but they are also able to meet with their lawyers and visitors, and appear before the immigration courts, in civilian clothing. Using Hutto and Berks as models, other immigration detention

facilities could—and should—allow detainees to wear their own clothing.

The 2009 DHS-ICE report recommended that discussion on the drafting of new detention standards and operating procedures should focus on a range of assumptions, including those relating to dress.[259] Indeed, ICE's Statement of Objectives calls for "[n]on-institutional detainee clothing and staff uniforms" in new facilities, but it appears that ICE interprets this provision to preclude prison jumpsuits, but allow more casual but still uniform clothing. For example, at ICA-Farmville, detainees are issued loose jeans with elastic waistbands and large blue or white t-shirts.[260] According to its contract, ICE detainees at the new facility in Karnes County "may be dressed in relaxed, non-traditional clothing."[261] ICE has told Human Rights First that detainees at Delaney Hall and Essex County jail in New Jersey will wear khaki pants and t-shirts.[262] In the first few days of operation at Delaney, however, ICE detainees were wearing lime-green prison jumpsuits.

Medical experts have concluded that wearing prison uniforms has a detrimental effect on detained asylum seekers. After conducting a comprehensive review of the impact of detention on asylum seekers, Physicians for Human Rights and the Bellevue/NYU Program for Survivors of Torture recommended that detained asylum seekers be permitted to wear their own clothing as a "simple, yet important" way for them to be "able to identify themselves as individuals and not as criminals."[263]

International authorities have also expressed concern about the U.S. practice of requiring detained asylum seekers and immigrants to wear prison uniforms. The U.N. Special Rapporteur on the Human Rights of Migrants has stressed that "[a]dministrative detention should never be of a punitive nature."[264] In a March 2008 report following a visit to the United States, the Special Rapporteur expressed concern about the punitive and "prison-like" nature of detention for immigration detainees in the United States, concluding that "[t]he conditions and terms of their detention are often prison-like: freedom of movement is restricted and detainees wear prison uniforms and are kept in a punitive setting."[265] In its major study on the U.S. immigration detention system, released in 2010, the Inter-American Commission on Human Rights also recommended to the U.S. government that "[d]etainees should be allowed to wear their own clothing."[266] Even in the case of non-migrants held on criminal charges pre-trial, the U.N. Standard Minimum Rules for the Treatment of Prisoners provide that "[a]n untried prisoner shall be allowed to wear his own clothing if it is clean and suitable."[267]

3) Contact visits

All ICE-authorized facilities should permit contact visits for all ICE detainees. ICE should ensure that the visitation schedule allows visitors traveling a distance ample time to spend with their detained family members or friends, during both weekends and weekdays, and that visitors are not forced to wait unreasonable periods of time for lack of adequate visitation space. Video visitation should not be used as a substitute for in-person visits.

At most of the 254 ICE-authorized detention facilities, detainees are not regularly permitted contact visitation with their families and friends. Visitors and detainees— many who have lived in the United States for many years, and have families and extended communities here, as well as others who have fled brutal persecution in their homelands and were locked up upon arrival in the United States—instead must sit on either side of a Plexiglas window and speak via telephone.[268] In several facilities, "visits" take place only via video, even when visitors are in the same building as detainees.[269] As the DHS-ICE report noted, "family visitation is often limited to noncontact visits of fairly short duration."[270] At some immigration detention facilities, visitation hours are severely limited.[271]

Current ICE standards leave it up to the facility administrator or officer in charge to decide whether to permit contact visits.[272] Human Rights First has identified just ten ICE-authorized facilities, out of 254, that regularly permit contact visitation; some others permit contact visitation under special circumstances, but not on a regular basis.[273] Dr. Schriro recommended that family visitation be improved by, among other things, increasing the hours and providing "appropriate space."[274] ICE's Statement of Objectives also calls for "[c]ontact visitation, including arrangements for visiting families, with extended hours."

The American Bar Association's Criminal Justice Standards on Treatment of Prisoners also provide for "contact visits between prisoners and their visitors," and "adequate" visiting time.[275] Contact visits—during which inmates can hold hands with their family members, and

embrace at the beginning and end of the visit—are permitted in jails and prisons across the country, including:

- New York City Department of Correction[276]
- New York State county jails and penitentiaries[277]
- Prison systems of all 50 states[278]
- All federal Bureau of Prisons facilities, holding in total more than 200,000 federal inmates[279]

Contact visits for immigration detainees would mean that they could embrace their family and friends in greeting and goodbye, and sit side by side while they visit. Loved ones could hold hands. Detained fathers and mothers would be able to touch their babies. Children would be able to hug their detained parents.

Corrections experts have affirmed the value of contact visits for incarcerated individuals.[280] A major 2006 report examining U.S. prison and jail systems at the request of Congress stated: "Because contact visits can inspire good behavior, people confined in both prisons and jails should be allowed to touch and embrace their children, partners, and other friends and family. Physical barriers and telephones should be reserved for those who have abused visitation privileges or otherwise have been determined to pose too great a risk."[281]

Human Rights First researchers spoke with some wardens and ICE assistant field officers who expressed concern that permitting contact visits would make a facility vulnerable to contraband passed between visitor and detainee, and that they would have to institute strip searches for detainees who had contact visits. However, Martin Horn, who ran the corrections systems in Pennsylvania and New York City, and Jeanne Woodford, the former San Quentin warden, both emphasized that strip searches following contact visits should take place only in cases of "reasonable cause or suspicion" or "high-risk inmates." They noted that screening technology can help decrease the use of actual strip searches.

4) Privacy in showers and toilets

All ICE facilities should provide some degree of privacy in showers and toilets for all ICE detainees. Open-bay (or "gang") showers and toilets should not be used for civil detainees.

Many ICE-authorized facilities afford no privacy whatsoever to detainees taking showers or using the toilet.[282] Yet according to an official who previously served with the Texas Department of Corrections, privacy in showers and toilets is available in "huge number of penal jails and prisons." "Gang showers"—open-bay shower areas with many showerheads—are "absolutely inappropriate."[283]

Human Rights First researchers spoke with some immigration detention facility administrators who cited safety concerns to justify the utter absence of privacy, but in fact many ICE and non-ICE facilities afford detainees the basic dignity of visual privacy in toilets and showers, without incident. Horn, who ran the corrections systems of Pennsylvania and New York City, said that partial barriers, from knee to neck, can be used to reduce the risk of suicides or sexual assault.[284] Another longtime corrections expert told Human Rights First that "privacy screens can be used that allow staff to see at least heads and/or feet in shower and/or toilet areas while still providing some level of privacy. Security concerns should not require that showers and toilets be completely open to staff observation, which implicitly means observation by other detainees as well."[285] At Essex County jail, which holds hundreds of ICE detainees with criminal histories, toilet stalls have full-length doors, and showers have tear-away curtains (designed to prevent self-strangulation). The jail warden says that the facility has never had problems with this set-up, and that the shower curtains are commonly used in criminal facilities.[286] The ABA Criminal Justice Standards call for "reasonably private" toilets for prisoners.[287]

Privacy in showers would require installation of Velcro tear-away shower curtains or opaque doors. Privacy in toilets would require installation of half- or full-length doors similar to the type used in public bathrooms. In both cases, dividers should be installed between each shower and toilet. Sinks should not be part of the toilet unit.

5) True outdoor recreation with expanded access

All ICE facilities should have outdoor recreation areas that are actually outside, accessible to detainees throughout the day, with dedicated space for sports and other physical activities, as well as grassy and shaded areas to allow for outdoor access during very hot or inclement weather. Fresh air and natural light should not be blocked. The size of the outdoor area or areas should be appropriate to the size of the detainee population.

At present, many facilities where immigrants are detained have no outdoor recreation space, or the space considered "outdoor" is in fact interior to the facility, enclosed by high cement walls and a cage-like ceiling through which some light and air can enter. In other facilities, the outdoor recreation area may be outdoors, but it is otherwise deficient—lacking shade or grass in extremely hot and sunny climates, or, in one case, plagued by poor air quality from neighboring industrial plants. [288] The current detention standards permit ICE to hold detainees in facilities without outdoor recreation "in exceptional circumstances." Where outdoor recreation exists, the requirements state that detainees must have access to it for just one hour per day, five days per week[289]—very little time for detained individuals with limited activities with which to fill their days.

The U.S. government itself has recognized the need for true and adequate outdoor recreation spaces at detention facilities. The DHS-ICE report flagged the importance of improving access to recreation, including outdoor recreation.[290] In its response to a draft of the 2010 report of the Inter-American Commission on Human Rights, the government confirmed its commitment to address the deficiency as part of its detention reform efforts: "The expansion of outdoor recreation opportunities and hours is an important part of the detention reform initiative. Detainees should have the opportunity to recreate for the most practicable amount of time possible in an environment that supports leisure activities and outdoor sports and exercise."[291] The ICE Statement of Objectives calls for "[e]nhanced ... outdoor recreational activities, with extended hours. Ideally, a minimum of four hours per day of outdoor recreation should be provided in a natural setting that allows for vigorous aerobic exercise."

Corrections professionals and ICE facility administrators have also acknowledged the benefits of outdoor recreation. The *Sheriff's Guide to Effective Jail Operations*, published by the National Institute of Corrections, states: "In addition to being beneficial for inmate health, the availability of outdoor and indoor exercise may result in fewer operational problems such as inmate-on-inmate assaults, inmate assaults on staff, damage to jail property, and lawsuits."[292] The former warden of a medium-security federal prison said in an interview, "We do surveys every year, and they show that as inmates get more involved in the [outdoor] rec program, they get in less trouble."[293] One ICE assistant field office director told Human Rights First that the better the recreation is, "the more likely they'll leave you alone."[294] A former prison official told us that outdoor recreation areas should have dedicated spaces for sports and other activities, rather than being just barren yards enclosed by fencing.[295] The ABA's Criminal Justice Standards on Treatment of Prisoners provide that, "To the extent practicable and consistent with prisoner and staff safety, correctional authorities should minimize the periods during the day in which prisoners are required to remain in their cells. Correctional authorities should provide all prisoners daily opportunities for significant out-of-cell time and for recreation at appropriate hours that allows them to maintain physical health and, for prisoners not in segregated housing, to socialize with other prisoners."[296]

Some ICE-authorized facilities already have appropriate outdoor recreation space, which should be used as models for other facilities.

Krome North Service Processing Center (Florida): The outdoor recreation area at Krome should be considered a model. The facility holds 567 male detainees. Its outdoor recreation area contains two soccer fields, a volleyball court, four basketball hoops, and picnic tables under a roof that provides shelter from the sun or during inclement weather, as well as additional open grassy areas.[297]

Broward Transitional Center (Florida): BTC holds 557 male and female detainees. Its courtyard/outdoor recreation space consists of a small sandy field for soccer, a volleyball court, a small covered area with exercise machines, a couple dozen tables under umbrellas, and another row of exercise machines, including a punching bag. Male detainees have access to the courtyard from 6am until sunset.[298] This layout could be replicated elsewhere.

T. Don Hutto Residential Center (Texas): Hutto holds up to 486 female detainees. The facility's outdoor recreation area is spacious, and includes picnic tables, a soccer field, a volleyball court, shaded areas, and grass. Detainees have access to the outdoors 12 hours per day.

James A. Musick Detention Facility (California): Musick holds 235 detainees. Its outdoor recreation area is accessible to detainees directly from their housing units at all times, except during meals and counts, which allows for between four and five hours every day. The

men's recreation area includes trees, benches, a soccer field, a volleyball court, and a basketball court, with a pleasant view of farmlands and mountains. The women's recreation area has a park-like feel to it with grass, trees, benches and a shaded space with a ping-pong table.

6) Programming and activities

ICE should ensure all detainees have access to daily programming and activities, including email.

According to corrections professionals, programming for incarcerated individuals helps to ensure safety inside a detention facility. For example, the *Sheriff's Guide to Effective Jail Operations,* published by the National Institute of Corrections, states: "Productive activities provide a powerful incentive for inmates to maintain positive behavior.... If a jail does not provide inmates with productive activities, they will find other ways to fill their time, often through activities that are destructive and contrary to the jail's mission of providing a safe and secure environment."[299] A national bipartisan commission created to examine violence in the U.S. prison and jail systems and make recommendations to improve safety for prisoners, staff, and the public stated in its 2006 report that "few conditions compromise safety more than idleness."[300]

Phone service in detention facilities is unreliable, extremely expensive, and appears to have improved only marginally despite ongoing concerns at the Government Accountability Office and the DHS Office of the Inspector General.[301] Given that email communication has become a primary form of communication for people all over the world, it would make sense for ICE facilities to provide email access to its detainees. All facilities operated by the federal Bureau of Prisons have an email system that is available to inmates at all security levels. Known as TRULINCS, this system permits inmates to send emails to and receive emails from a preapproved list of contacts.[302] The only immigration detention facility visited by Human Rights First that permits email access is T. Don Hutto Residential Center, where detainees may access Internet for 30 minutes per day, and they use their time primarily to text with their family.[303] Delaney Hall, the new facility in New Jersey, is also slated to provided limited email access, according to ICE. Martin, the former General Counsel of the Texas prison system, contended that immigration detainees should have access to the Internet as well as email. He said, "The risk is minimal with proper controls, and the benefits would be enormous in facilitating communication with family and attorneys."[304]

ICE's new guidance on the use of prosecutorial discretion by ICE personnel, coupled with the Administration's plans to review 300,000 cases in removal proceedings, including detained cases, and administratively close the cases of low-priority individuals, may change the composition of the detained population in the future, decreasing the proportion of immigration detainees without criminal records. However, even if such a decrease happens, it would not change the need to shift the detention system away from the current jail model toward conditions more appropriate for civil immigration detainees. As described above, normalized conditions

have been linked to safety in facilities holding higher-risk as well as low-risk detainees. An effective and standardized assessment tool can identify individuals who may pose a risk to officers or to other detainees, and in such cases, ICE can ensure appropriate placement separate from lower-risk detainees, or other measures proportionate to the risk, to improve safety. Furthermore, if ICE does increase the proportion of its detained population with criminal records, that population would not necessarily pose a greater risk to facility safety. An individual's criminal record may include only a non-violent crime, or a standardized risk assessment tool may determine that an individual with a criminal record would not pose a risk to facility safety, as criminal history is just one factor in such an assessment.

Recommendations and Next Steps

The U.S. Department of Homeland Security and Immigration and Customs Enforcement should move forward with their commitments to transform the immigration detention system away from its reliance on prisons, jails, and jail-like facilities that are inappropriate for detaining asylum seekers and other civil immigration law detainees. Some critical next steps are outlined below.

More broadly, the United States should bring its laws, policies, and practices relating to immigration detention in line with international standards and U.S. traditions of fairness. The United States has pledged itself to abide by the commitments outlined in the 1951 Convention Relating to the Status of Refugees—which celebrates its 60th anniversary this year—its Protocol, as well as the International Covenant on Civil and Political Rights, which prohibits arbitrary detention and requires independent court review of detention decisions.

ICE should not detain asylum seekers or other immigrants without a fair and individualized assessment of the need to detain. Under international standards, asylum seekers should generally not be detained.[305] Immigration detention should have adequate safeguards, including procedures to ensure custody review by an independent authority or court.[306] In many cases, asylum seekers and other immigration detainees should be released from detention on parole or through an immigration court custody hearing if they meet the applicable criteria, or released to a supervised release program, or other Alternative to Detention program, if some supervision of the release is necessary. When asylum seekers and other immigrants are detained, they should not be held in jails or jail-like facilities. Instead, ICE should ensure that the conditions of their detention are non-penal in nature and appropriate to their status as immigration detainees, as detailed in this report.

Thorough reform of the U.S. detention system will require a combination of legislative, regulatory, and administrative actions. We have outlined below a series of significant changes that will improve U.S. detention policies and practices in general and for the victims of persecution who seek this country's protection.

1. **Stop Using Prisons, Jails, and Jail-like Facilities.** Over the next two years, DHS and ICE should move forward on their commitments to transform the current detention system modeled on jails to one with conditions appropriate for civil immigration law detainees and end the use of extra bed space in county and state jails and prisons across the country to detain immigrants in ICE custody.

    a. **End the Use of Jails and Prisons.** As the agency moves forward in transforming the system, **Immigration and Customs Enforcement** should phase out contracts with county and state jails and prisons, which are inappropriate for civil immigration law detainees. ICE should also end the use of jail-like immigration detention facilities.

    b. **Use Facilities with More Appropriate Conditions.** After an individualized assessment of whether detention is necessary, when asylum seekers and other immigrants are detained under the civil immigration laws, they should not be held in prisons, jails, or jail-like facilities. Instead, **Immigration and Customs Enforcement** should use facilities with more appropriate conditions that provide a more normalized environment, permitting detainees to wear their own clothing, move freely among various areas within a secure facility and grounds, access true outdoor recreation for extended periods of time, access programming and email, have some privacy in toilets and showers, and have contact visits with family and friends. These more normalized conditions should exist for the vast majority of asylum seekers and other immigrants held in detention. As detailed in this report, normalized living conditions in detention can actually improve safety inside a facility and are considered by many corrections professionals to be a best practice of custody management even in the correctional context.

c. **Develop and Implement New Standards Specifying Conditions for Civil Immigration Detention. Immigration and Customs Enforcement** should develop new residential detention standards that require all facilities to include the key elements outlined in this report—including permitting detainees to wear their own clothing, move freely among various areas within a secure facility and grounds, access true outdoor recreation for extended periods of time, access programming and email, have some privacy in toilets and showers, and have contact visits with family and friends. To promote compliance, these new standards should be incorporated into contracts and promulgated into regulations.

d. **Reform Existing Immigration Detention Facilities to the Extent Possible.** While existing jail-like facilities remain inappropriate for civil immigration law detainees, some reforms can be implemented at these facilities while the transition to more appropriate facilities moves forward. In these existing detention facilities, **Immigration and Customs Enforcement** should ensure that contact visits, true and expanded outdoor recreation, and privacy for showers and toilets are instituted within six months wherever the physical plant does not preclude these reforms. The changes made since 2007 at Hutto Detention Center in Texas can serve as a model for reforms to existing facilities.

e. **Use Automated and Effective Risk Classification Assessment Tool to Identify and Properly Place Any Detainees Who Present Safety Risks in Custody. Immigration and Customs Enforcement** should complete the process of automating a risk classification assessment tool for use in all ICE-authorized facilities. In addition to identifying individuals who should be released, an effective and standardized assessment tool can identify individuals who may pose a risk to officers or to other detainees, and in such cases, ICE can ensure appropriate placement separate from lower-risk detainees, or other measures proportionate to the risk, to improve safety. In taking such measures, ICE should not automatically hold in a correctional setting all detainees with criminal convictions.[307] Further, a risk assessment tool is an important management tool—not a substitute for independent review of the need to detain.

2. **Prevent Unnecessary Costs by Ensuring that Asylum Seekers and Other Immigrants Are Not Detained Unnecessarily.** The creation of facilities with more appropriate conditions should not be used as a reason to detain individuals who present no risks and meet the requirements for release, including through an Alternative to Detention where additional supervision is necessary to ensure compliance.

f. **Expand Alternatives to Detention Nationwide.** When a detained asylum seeker or other immigrant is not eligible for release on parole, bond, or recognizance, and some additional supervision is determined to be necessary, the individual should be assessed for release to a supervised release program or other Alternative to Detention. To determine eligibility for release or ATDs, ICE should use an automated and effective risk classification assessment tool that recognizes the unique characteristics of a civilly detained immigration population. **Immigration and Customs Enforcement** should create an effective nationwide system of ATDs, utilizing full-service community-based models that provide individualized case management, increasing access to legal and social service providers through meaningful referrals, as well as access to information about court and case information. ICE should consider some forms of Alternatives to Detention to constitute custody for the purposes of the mandatory detention laws, and enroll detainees subject to mandatory detention who are otherwise eligible for release into those programs.

When used as true alternatives to detention for individuals who would not otherwise be released—and not as alternatives to release for the non-detained population in removal proceedings—ATD programs should create significant cost savings for the government—more than $110 per person per day. **Congress** should ensure that cost savings are realized in the expansion of this program by reallocating part of the detention and removal budget to an increase in the ATD budget. A nationwide system of Alternatives to Detention for individuals who would otherwise be detained would also bring U.S. policy into greater compliance with international human rights standards regarding detention.[308]

g. **Provide Immigration Court Custody Hearings for All Detainees.** The **Departments of Justice and Homeland Security** should revise regulatory language and/or **Congress** should enact legislation to provide arriving asylum seekers and other immigration detainees with the chance to have their custody reviewed in a hearing before an immigration court. Even with improved parole guidance, the absence of prompt, independent court review of decisions to detain arriving asylum seekers and other detained immigrants is inconsistent with U.S. obligations under the Refugee Convention and the International Covenant on Civil and Political Rights.[309]

h. **Revise Laws to Provide for Detention Only After Individualized Assessment of the Need to Detain. Congress** should revise laws so that an asylum seeker or other immigrant may be detained only after an assessment of the need for detention in his or her individual case, rather than through automatic or mandatory detention.[310]

3. **Improve Access to Legal Assistance and Fair Procedures.** DOJ, DHS, and ICE should work with Congress to ensure that detained asylum seekers and other immigration detainees have sufficient access to legal representation, legal information, and in-person hearings of their asylum claims and deportation cases.

a. **End Use of Facilities in Remote Locations So That Detainees Can Access Legal Representation, Medical Care, and Family.** All facilities holding ICE detainees should be located near an urban center that can offer

legal representation and medical and social services. The 2009 ICE-DHS report recommended that "facilities should be placed nearby consulates, pro bono counsel, EOIR services, asylum offices, and 24-hour emergency medical care" and that the "system should be linked by transportation."[311] Yet according to Human Rights First calculations, 40 percent of all ICE bed space is currently more than 60 miles from an urban center. **Immigration and Customs Enforcement** should end the use of all facilities in remote locations to help ensure that detainees can access not only attorneys, but also their families, doctors, psychiatrists and psychologists, and social services.[312]

b. **Ensure that Legal Orientation Presentations (LOPs) Are Funded and in Place at All Facilities That Detain Asylum Seekers or Other Immigration Detainees.** The **Department of Justice,** the **White House,** and **Congress** should work together to ensure that LOPs are fully funded at all ICE-authorized facilities used to detain asylum seekers and other immigrants. While not a substitute for legal counsel, these presentations promote fundamental fairness and improve the efficiency of the courts. **Immigration and Customs Enforcement** should not detain immigrants in new facilities until LOP funding to serve those facilities is in place.

c. **Ensure that In-Person Immigration Judges and Asylum Officers Are Available for All Detained Asylum Seekers or Other Immigration Detainees. Immigration and Customs Enforcement, the Executive Office of Immigration Review, U.S. Citizenship and Immigration Services,** and **Congress** should work together to ensure that in-person immigration judge and asylum officer staffing is in place to cover the detained docket and CFI/RFI needs without the use of video-conference. The **Department of Justice's Executive Office for Immigration Review** should ensure adequate staffing and resources so that all merits hearings can be conducted in person rather than via video-conference. **Congress** should appropriate adequate funding to both the immigration courts and the asylum office so that they can conduct merits hearings and hear asylum claims in person rather than by video.

4. **Take Other Steps to Address Deficiencies in Immigration Detention Conditions.** Though ICE has taken some steps toward improving conditions in the existing system, serious deficiencies persist. DHS and ICE should implement a number of improvements in all facilities housing immigration detainees, including:

   a. **Ensure High-Quality Medical and Mental Health Treatment**: The **Department of Homeland Security** and **Immigration and Customs Enforcement** should take additional steps to improve the timely provision of medical and mental health treatment at all facilities where asylum seekers and other immigration detainees are held. They should continue to seek input from independent experts and medical professionals, many of whom have provided detailed recommendations on improving medical and mental health treatment in immigration detention facilities.[313]

   b. **Adopt Bipartisan Rape and Abuse Prevention Standards**: The **Departments of Homeland Security, Justice,** and **Health and Human Services** should ensure that all facilities holding immigration detainees are covered by the standards, including the supplemental immigration detention standards, developed by the bipartisan federal National Prison Rape Elimination Commission, as clearly intended by the Commission and the legislation that created it.[314]

   c. **Improve Training and Communication**. **Immigration and Customs Enforcement** should ensure that all officers and facility staff interacting with ICE detainees throughout the detention system—whether employed by ICE, local jails or prisons, or private contractors— receive in-depth training annually on the particular situation and needs of an immigrant detainee population, among other training and professional development opportunities. The **DHS Office of Civil Rights and Civil Liberties** should support this training. In the criminal detention context, experts have emphasized that reforms to a physical environment must be accompanied with appropriate staff training on how to work under new conditions and expectations.[315] Corrections experts have also asserted the need for "professional correctional leadership" in order to effect lasting improvement in a prison system; their recommendation for high-quality recruitment and training of facility staff and managers should apply equally to those working in immigration detention facilities.[316] ICE should also ensure that reform policies and priorities developed at headquarters are communicated to, and implemented by, local staff, and that experiences from the field inform ICE policies created in Washington. Specifically, ICE should send formal guidance on how to conduct reforms to its field offices and all staff working in facilities, whether they are employed by ICE, local jails or prisons, or private contractors.

Appendix

Sample ICE Statement of Objectives

Enforcement and Removal Operations

U.S. Department of Homeland Security
101 W. Congress Parkway, Suite 400
Chicago, IL 60605

**U.S. Immigration
and Customs
Enforcement**

September 10, 2010

Dear Sheriff:

A key goal of Immigration Detention Reform is to create a civil detention system that is not penal in nature. However, Immigration and Customs Enforcement (ICE) recognizes that some detainees may have a criminal history. Consequently, detainees at the medium and maximum classification levels may require housing in a more secure area of the facility. The new system will provide safe and secure conditions of confinement based on the individual characteristics of a diverse population, including: threat to the community, risk of flight, type and status of immigration proceeding, community ties, medical and mental health issues. Accordingly, ICE requires a wholly new generation of detention facilities uniquely suited to ICE's civil detention authority. The new facilities must feature innovative and cost-effective designs and new approaches to construction materials, staffing, and operations. They must also provide easy access to legal services, abundant natural light, ample outdoor recreation, contact visitation, noise control, freedom of movement, programming opportunities consistent with detainee demographics, and state-of-the art medical facilities.

The attached statement of objectives (SOO) reflects the need to acquire detention services from a law enforcement partner in a supervised facility that is safe and secure, prevents unauthorized entry and egress, and provides appropriate custody and care to the ICE detention population. In response to this SOO, interested law enforcement agencies should submit a written concept proposal or white paper to the Cognizant Contracting Officer and local ERO Field Office Director (FOD) on or before October 8, 2010, that provides an overview of the offeror's proposed facility and demonstrates how operation of that facility correlates to the ICE detention concept described in the SOO. An estimated per diem rate and estimated delivery time should also be included. If interested, please send your proposal to my attention at the address provide in the letterhead. If you have any questions concerning this SOO please contact Assistant Field Office Director Ken Carlson out of our Kansas City office at (816)880-5050.

Sincerely,

Ricardo A. Wong
Field Office Director

Attachments

STATEMENT OF OBJECTIVES
IMMIGRATION DETENTION REFORM
REQUEST FOR INTER-GOVERNMENTAL SERVICE AGREEMENT (IGSA)
CONCEPT PROPOSAL: CHICAGO

A. Introduction:

A key goal of Immigration Detention Reform is to create a civil detention system that is not penal in nature. However, ICE recognizes that some detainees may have a criminal history. Consequently, detainees at the medium and maximum classification levels may require housing in a more secure area of the facility. The new system will provide safe and secure conditions of confinement based on the individual characteristics of a diverse population, including: threat to the community, risk of flight, type and status of immigration proceeding, community ties, medical and mental health issues. Accordingly, ICE requires a wholly new generation of detention facilities uniquely suited to ICE's civil detention authority. The new facilities must feature innovative and cost-effective designs and new approaches to construction materials, staffing, and operations. They must also provide easy access to legal services, abundant natural light, ample outdoor recreation, contact visitation, noise control, freedom of movement, programming opportunities consistent with detainee demographics, and state-of-the art medical facilities.

This statement of objectives (SOO) reflects the need to acquire detention services from an IGSA partner in a supervised facility that is safe and secure, prevents unauthorized entry and egress, and provides appropriate custody and care to the ICE detention population specified below in Section B, Facility Overview. In response to this SOO, interested IGSA holders should submit a written concept proposal or white paper to the Cognizant Contracting Officer and local ERO Field Office Director (FOD) on or before September 30, 2010, that provides an overview of the offeror's proposed facility and demonstrates how operation of that facility correlates to the ICE detention concept described below. An estimated per diem rate and estimated delivery time should also be included.

The Government cannot guarantee that an award will be from these submissions.

B. Facility Overview:

The desired services can be provided in a dedicated or non-dedicated facility or campus with both secure (medium and maximum security cases) and non-secure residential (low and minimum security cases) beds that is designed and operated to process and house adult detainees, including the full range of criminal and non-criminal cases, in a manner consistent with ICE's recently announced civil detention reform initiatives.

The facility or campus must have a minimum of 125 detention beds for ICE utilization. The ideal facility will have 200—250 detention beds to house ICE detainees. Eighty percent of

Statement of Objectives (SOO): Request for IGSA Concept Proposal: North East
Page 2 of 4

capacity should be secure beds, and 20 percent of capacity should be non-secure beds. The facility or campus must have the ability to separately house male and female detainees of all ICE security classifications levels in accordance with the ICE Performance Based National Detention Standards (PBNDS).

The ideal facility or campus housing ICE detainees will have or offer the following:

Facility Exterior/Design:

- Innovative designs, materials, and technology that, where possible and practical, combine the use of innovative soft construction techniques with traditional "brick and mortar" penal structures, which will reduce construction and operating costs while promoting the least restrictive detention environments appropriate to the population.

- An environmentally sustainable design and operation that is certifiable through the Leadership in Energy and Environmental Design (LEED) process.

- Possible co-location with an existing detention facility that can provide or at least augment support services, such as: food, maintenance, laundry, utilities, and dental/medical/mental health as a way of minimizing construction costs, build-out time, and operational expenses.

- Infrastructure capability and flexibility to expand or contract bed space capacity as ICE detention demographics and population numbers fluctuate and shift (over the long-term).

- Appropriately sized and staffed dental, medical, and mental health facilities. The IGSA will arrange for a health services provider or may request ICE's Division of Immigration Health Services (DIHS) to staff and operate the medical unit.

- Video-conferencing capability for the Executive Office for Immigration Review (EOIR).

- Multiple Closed Circuit Television (CCTV) cameras and/or other appropriate electronic security equipment throughout the campus or facility, including all entry and exits points, all housing units, and all areas where detainees are authorized to move and congregate.

Facility Interior/Operations:

- Natural/ambient light throughout the facility.

- Indoor and outdoor community areas with durable, fire-resistant, non-institutional seating and furniture, and softer interior settings throughout the facility.

- Enhanced but controlled freedom of detainee movement. Freedom of movement will be applicable to all ICE classification levels, although the manner and degree of implementation may vary based on security levels.

Statement of Objectives (SOO): Request for IGSA Concept Proposal: North East
Page 3 of 4

- Enhanced indoor and outdoor recreational activities, with extended hours. Ideally, a minimum of four hours per day of outdoor recreation should be provided in a natural setting that allows for vigorous aerobic exercise.

- Enhanced programming, including religious services and social programs, as appropriate for the population demographics,

- Enhanced law library and legal resources.

- Dedicated space for religious services.

- Emphasis on communal areas and social interactions consistent with security levels.

- Contact visitation, including arrangements for visiting families, with extended hours. This will be applicable to all ICE classification levels, although the manner of implementation may vary based on security levels. Where practicable, visitation should include visitation both day and evening hours, seven days a week.

- Private areas for attorney-client contact visitation, video teleconferencing capability, and innovative solutions for visitation, including virtual visitation, from remote areas for attorneys and families unable to travel to the facility.

- Private showers and restrooms, where practicable and appropriate based on security levels.

- Cafeteria-style meal service with menu options. (Satellite feeding of detainees in certain secure areas or limited circumstances may be required, but should be limited).

- Non-institutional detainee clothing and staff uniforms.

- A high-degree of facility staff-detainee interaction in order to address detainee grievances, housing issues and facility concerns.

C. Facility Location:

The ideal facility location will:

- Be within a two-hour surface commute of the Chicago Field Office located at 101 W. Congress Parkway, Chicago, Illinois..

- Serve as a transportation hub for picking up and dropping off ICE detainees within an 8 hour one way drive time from the facility.

Statement of Objectives (SOO): Request for IGSA Concept Proposal: North East
Page 4 of 4

- Be within an approximate 30-minute surface commute time of a general acute care hospital that has an emergency room, surgery, medical, and mental health services and within an approximate 90-minute surface commute time of an ICE/DRO Air Operations Unit-approved airport.

- Have access to public and commercial transportation routes and services.

- Have access to local consulates and pro-bono legal services.

D. Performance Outcomes

Expected Outcomes may be viewed at the following three links:

Performance-Based National Detention Standards (PBNDS)
The more restrictive, secure areas will be governed by the optimal performance levels articulated in the ICE PBNDS 2008 (currently in existence) or 2010 (pending approval), available at the following website: http://www.ice.gov/partners/dro/PBNDS 2010/index.htm .

Adult Residential Standards (ARS)
The non-secure residential areas will be governed by the performance levels articulated in the ICE Adult Residential Standards available at the following website: http://www.ice.gov/partners/dro/ARS2010/index.htm . The ARS are currently under development.

Endnotes

1   John Morton, Assistant Secretary, Immigration and Customs Enforcement, Migration Policy Institute Speakers Series—Leadership Visions, Washington, DC, January 25, 2010. Transcript on file with Human Rights First.

2   Nina Bernstein, "Ideas for Immigrant Detention Include Converting Hotels and Building Models," New York Times, October 5, 2009.

3   DHS/ICE, *Endgame: Office of Detention and Removal Strategic Plan, 2003-2012* (June 2003), p. 2-11.

4   Office of Immigration Statistics—Policy Directorate, Department of Homeland Security, *Immigration Enforcement Actions: 2010* (Washington, DC: DHS, 2011), p. 1.

5   UNHCR, UNHCR's Revised Guidelines on Applicable Criteria and Standards Related to the Detention of Asylum Seekers, February 26, 1999, Guideline 5(iii) (xx), available at http://www.unhcr.org/refworld/docid/3c2b3f844.html (accessed September 27, 2011); U.N. Commission on Human Rights Working Group on Arbitrary Detention, *Report of the Working Group on Arbitrary Detention*, principle 9, (1999), E/CN.4/2000/4., p. 30; Gabriel Rodriguez Pizarro, UN Special Rapporteur on the Human Rights of Migrants, *Report of the Special Rapporteur on the Human Rights of Migrants* (Geneva: UNHCR, 2002), E/CN.4/2003/85., ¶ 54 ("[a]dministrative detention should never be of a punitive nature.") (hereinafter cited as 2002 UN Special Rapporteur Report); Organization of American States, Inter-American Commission on Human Rights, *Report on Immigration in the United States: Detention and Due Process*, OEA/Ser.L/V/II. Doc 78/10, December 30, 2010, ¶ 19, p. 6 (The Commission was "troubled by the lack of a genuinely civil detention system.") (hereinafter cited as IACHR Report).

6   Mark Dow, *American Gulag: Inside U.S. Immigration Prisons*, Berkeley: University of California Press, 2004, p. 229-36.

7   Dr. Dora Schriro, *Immigration Detention Overview and* Recommendations (Washington, DC: Immigration and Customs Enforcement, 2009), p. 2-3, available at http://www.ice.gov/doclib/about/offices/odpp/pdf/ice-detention-rpt.pdf. (hereinafter cited as 2009 DHS/ICE Report) ("The purpose of immigration detention is "to hold, process, and prepare individuals for removal.") citing *Zadvydas v. Davis*, 533 U.S. 678, 609 (2001) (Immigration proceedings are civil proceedings and immigration detention is not punishment.); e.g. Intergovernmental Service Agreement Between the United States Department of Homeland Security, U.S. Immigration and Customs Enforcement, Office of Enforcement and Removal Operations, and the City of Adelanto, EROIGSA-11-2003, signed May 13, 2011 and May 27, 2011, p. 2 (hereinafter cited as Adelanto IGSA). This and several other IGSAs were obtained by Human Rights First through a public information request. ("All persons in the custody of ICE are 'Administrative Detainees.' This term recognizes that ICE detainees are not charged with criminal violations and are only held in custody to assure their presence throughout the administrative hearing process and to assure their presence for removal from the United States pursuant to a lawful final order by the Immigration Court, the Board of Immigration Appeals or other Federal judicial body.")

8   US Commission on International Religious Freedom, *Asylum Seekers in Expedited Removal, Volume I: Findings & Recommendations* (Washington, DC: USCIRF, 2005), p. 189; US Commission on International Religious Freedom, *Expedited Removal Study Report Card: Two Years Later* (Washington, DC: USCIRF, 2007), p. 5.

9   USCIRF, *Asylum Seekers in Expedited Removal*, p. 189.

10 ICE opened or began using the following detention facilities between the time that the Commission's report was released (February 2005), and the time that Human Rights First's report was released (April 2009): South Texas Detention Center (1,904 beds), Willacy Detention Center (3,000 beds), Stewart Detention Center (1,524 beds), T. Don Hutto Family Detention Center (512 beds), Bristol Detention Center (128 beds), LaSalle/Jena Detention Center (1,160 beds), and Otero County Processing Center (1,088 beds).

11 Human Rights First calculations based on data provided by the ICE Office of State, Local, and Tribal Coordination, on file with Human Rights First. Level 1s—low-risk detainees, according to ICE—include detainees with minor criminal records or nonviolent felonies, but do not include detainees with violent felony or aggravated felony convictions. Level 2s—medium-risk detainees—may not include detainees whose most recent conviction was for a severe offense, or detainees with a pattern or history of violent assaults, whether convicted or not. ICE/DRO Detention Standard, "Classification System." All non-criminals should be classified as Level 1s, but it appears from this data that is not the case.

12 Data received through a Freedom of Information Act request to ICE, on file with Human Rights First. Categories are not mutually exclusive.

13 2009 DHS/ICE Report, p. 2.

14 Correspondence with senior ICE officials, October 1, 2011.

15 USCIRF letter to Stewart Baker.

16 Council on Foreign Relations Independent Task Force on U.S. Immigration Policy, *Independent Task Force Report No. 63—U.S. Immigration Policy* (New York: CFR, 2009), p. 32 (hereinafter cited as CFR Report on Immigration Policy).

[17] Constitution Project, *Recommendations for Reforming Our Immigration Detention System and Promoting Access to Counsel in Immigration Proceedings* (Washington, DC: Constitution Project, 2009), p. 1.

[18] See, e.g. Physicians for Human Rights, "Dual Loyalties: The Challenges of Providing Professional Health Care to Immigration Detainees," March 2011; DHS Office of the Inspector General, *Management of Mental Health Cases in Immigration Detention*, OIG-11-62 (Washington, DC: DHS, March 2011), available at http://www.dhs.gov/xoig/assets/mgmtrpts/OIG_11-62_Mar11.pdf; Texas Appleseed, *Justice for Immigration's Hidden Population: Protecting the Rights of Persons with Mental Disabilities in the Immigration Court and Detention System* (Austin: Texas Appleseed, 2010), available at http://www.texasappleseed.net/index.php?option=com_docman&task=doc_download&gid=313&Itemid.; DHS Office of the Inspector General, *The U.S. Immigration and Customs Enforcement Process for Authorizing Medical Care for Immigration Detainees* (Washington, DC: DHS Office of the Inspector General, 2009); Florida Immigrant Advocacy Center, *Dying for Decent Care: Bad Medicine in Immigration Custody* (Miami: FIAC, 2009); Human Rights Watch, *Detained and Dismissed: Women's Struggles to Obtain Health Care in United States Immigration Detention* (New York: Human Rights Watch, 2009); Amnesty International, *Jailed Without Justice*;" Amy Goldstein and Dana Priest, "In Custody, In Pain," *Washington Post*, May 12, 2008; Physicians for Human Rights and Bellevue/NYU Program for Survivors of Torture, *From Persecution to Prison: The Health Consequences of Detention for Asylum Seekers* (New York: Physicians for Human Rights and Bellevue/NYU Program for Survivors of Torture, 2003).

[19] CQ Newsmaker Transcripts, "Immigration and Customs Enforcement Assistant Secretary John Morton Holds Conference Call to Announce Major Reforms Planned for the Immigration Detention System," August 6, 2009, available at http://homeland.cq.com/hs/display.do?docid=3189020, transcript on file with Human Rights First.

[20] In 2010 and 2011, Human Rights First researchers received tours from ICE and county jail officials and private contractors at the following detention facilities: Northwest Detention Center (Tacoma, WA), El Centro Service Processing Center (El Centro, CA), James A. Musick Facility (Orange County, CA), Theo Lacy Facility (Orange County, CA), Otero County Processing Center (Chaparral, NM), T. Don Hutto Residential Center (Taylor, TX), South Texas Detention Complex (Pearsall, TX), Willacy Detention Center (Raymondville, TX), Port Isabel Detention Center (Los Fresnos, TX), Glades County Detention Center (Moore Haven, FL), Krome North Service Processing Center (Miami, FL), Broward Transitional Center (Pompano Beach, FL), Immigration Centers of America—Farmville (Farmville, VA), Berks Family Detention Center (Leesport, PA), Elizabeth Detention Center (Elizabeth, NJ), Essex County Jail (Newark, NJ), and Hudson County Jail (Kearny, NJ).

[21] They were classified by ICE as "Level 1s" or "low Level 2s." Level 1s—low-risk detainees, according to ICE—include detainees with minor criminal records or nonviolent felonies, but do not include detainees with violent felony or aggravated felony convictions. Level 2s—medium-risk detainees—may not include detainees whose most recent conviction was for a severe offense, or detainees with a pattern or history of violent assaults, whether convicted or not. ICE/DRO Detention Standard, "Classification System."

[22] *Fiscal 2011 Appropriations: Homeland* Security, *Before the Senate Appropriations Comm.*, 111th Cong. (March 18, 2010) (2010) (testimony of John Morton, Assistant Secretary, Immigration and Customs Enforcement), available at http://www.dhs.gov/ynews/testimony/testimony_1271443011074.shtm.

[23] "DHS, "Secretary Napolitano Appoints Dora Schriro as Special Advisor on ICE and Detention & Removal," news release February 4, 2009, available at http://www.dhs.gov/ynews/releases/pr_1233777219314.shtm. For US government criticism of America's immigration detention system, see, e.g. DHS Office of the Inspector General, *Management of Mental Health Cases*; .

[24] See 2009 DHS/ICE Report.

[25] Supra, note 19; ICE, "Fact Sheet: 2009 Immigration Detention Reforms," available at http://www.ice.gov/news/library/factsheets/reform-2009reform.htm.

[26] ICE's 2010-2014 strategic plan made a related commitment—to "reduce reliance on excess capacity in State and local penal facilities." ICE, *ICE Strategic Plan FY 2010-2014* (Washington, DC: ICE, 2010), p. 6 (hereinafter cited as ICE 2010-2014 Strategic Plan).

[27] ICE, "Fact Sheet: ICE Detention Reform Principles and Next Steps," news release, October 6, 2009, available at http://www.dhs.gov/xlibrary/assets/press_ice_detention_reform_fact_sheet.pdf; DHS press conference, October 6, 2009, video recording, http://www.c-spanvideo.org/program/289313-1.

[28] ICE's 2010-2014 strategic plan made a related commitment—to "apply new detention standards to existing facilities" within the following five fiscal years. ICE 2010-2014 Strategic Plan, p. 6.

[29] 2009 DHS/ICE Report, p. 2-3.

[30] *A Report on the Preliminary Assessment of ICE Detention Policies and Practices and A Recommended Course of Action for Systems Reform, Before the House Homeland Sec. Comm., Subcomm. on Border, Maritime, and Global Counterterrorism*, 111th Cong. (December 10, 2009) (written testimony of Dr. Dora Schriro, Commissioner of the New York City Dept. of Correction) (hereinafter cited as Schriro testimony, *Preliminary Assessment*); 2009 DHS/ICE Report, p. 3, 18-19, 22..

[31] 2009 DHS/ICE Report, p. 23-24..

[32] Schriro testimony, *Preliminary Assessment*; 2009 DHS/ICE Report, p. 23.

[33] Morton, MPI Speakers Series.

[34] In 2005, a prison expert retained by the U.S. Commission on International Religious Freedom enumerated some specific conditions that made ICE facilities prison-like, including the use of correctional models of security, surveillance, and control, including multiple daily inmate headcounts; restricted movement and segregated confinement; limitations on privacy and personal freedom; requirements to wear uniforms rather than street clothes; restrictions on access to programming and meaningful activity; and limitations on contact with the outside world. USCIRF, *Asylum Seekers in Expedited Removal*, p. 185-89. In 2009, Dr. Schriro confirmed that "[a]ll but a few of the facilities that ICE uses to detain aliens were built as jails and prisons." She described them: "Quite a few do not have windows. A number consist of single and double celled units and others are dormitories of varying size. Movement is largely restricted and detainees spend the majority of time in their housing units. A recreation area is often adjacent to the housing unit and meals are served in the dayroom in quite a few locations, not in a separate dining hall. Access to recreation, religious services, the law library, and visitation can be improved. Segregation cells are often used for purposes other than discipline." 2009 DHS/ICE Report, p. 21. In 2010, the Inter-American Commission on Human Rights stated that the facilities it visited all "employ[ed] disproportionally restrictive penal and punitive measures." IACHR described conditions where "detained immigrants wear prison uniforms; all the units operate as incarceration facilities; on a daily basis detainees are subjected to multiple head counts that require that they remain in their beds for as much as an hour at a time; the prison guards sometimes lock them in (confine them to their cells or force them to stay in their beds); and detainees are handcuffed and shackled whenever they are taken outside the center's walls, even when they are taken to court." IACHR Report, ¶ 246, p. 86..

[35] 2009 DHS/ICE Report, p. 10.

[36] In FY11, according to ICE data, approximately 47 percent of the average daily detained population (14,934 out of 31,653) was being held in non-dedicated or shared-use facilities—i.e. correctional facilities that either have an ICE section within the larger facility, or that actually co-mingle ICE detainees with regular criminal pre-trial detainees and/or sentenced criminals, depending on the facility. For example, in Glades County Detention Center (Moore Haven, FL), run by the Glades County Sheriff's Office, ICE detainees are held in separate pods, and do not mix with county inmates, but the facility itself is inarguably a well-run jail. At York County Prison (York, PA), on the other hand, according to an ICE detainee who was held there, as well as volunteers who provide services there, immigrants detained for more than two weeks are mixed in with the state inmate population. At Hudson County Correctional Facility (Kearny, NJ), ICE detainees are co-mingled with county and U.S. Marshal detainees in all areas except housing. According to an informal survey by Human Rights First, facilities that actually co-mingle ICE detainees with regular inmates include Ramsey Jail (Minnesota), Cumberland County Jail (Maine), York County Prison (Pennsylvania), Douglas County Corrections (Nevada), Rappahannock (Virginia), Hampton Roads Jail (Virginia), Mecklenberg County Jail (Charlotte, NC), Monmouth County Jail (NJ), and Boone County Jail (IL). In its 2009 report on America's immigration system, Amnesty International listed 16 facilities where ICE co-mingled its detainees with criminal inmates; 8 of these facilities continue to hold ICE detainees. (Amnesty International, *Jailed Without Justice: Immigration Detention in the USA*, (New York: Amnesty International, 2009), note 134, p. 52).

[37] Dedicated ICE facilities include six Service Processing Centers, seven Contract Detention Facilities, and seven dedicated IGSA facilities, which together on held on average 16,719 or 53 percent of the ICE daily detention population in FY 2011, according to ICE data as of 7/18/11.

[38] ICE, "Fact Sheet: 2009 Immigration Detention Reforms."

[39] In 2010 and 2011, Human Rights First researchers received tours from ICE and county jail officials and private contractors at the following detention facilities: Northwest Detention Center (Tacoma, WA), El Centro Service Processing Center (El Centro, CA), James A. Musick Facility (Orange County, CA), Theo Lacy Facility (Orange County, CA), Otero County Processing Center (Chaparral, NM), T. Don Hutto Residential Center (Taylor, TX), South Texas Detention Complex (Pearsall, TX), Willacy Detention Center (Raymondville, TX), Port Isabel Detention Center (Los Fresnos, TX), Glades County Detention Center (Moore Haven, FL), Krome North Service Processing Center (Miami, FL), Broward Transitional Center (Pompano Beach, FL), Immigration Centers of America—Farmville (Farmville, VA), Berks Family Detention Center (Leesport, PA), Elizabeth Detention Center (Elizabeth, NJ), Essex County Jail (Newark, NJ), and Hudson County Jail (Kearny, NJ).

[40] They were classified by ICE as "level 1s" or "low level 2s." Level 1s—low-risk detainees, according to ICE—include detainees with minor criminal records or nonviolent felonies, but do not include detainees with violent felony or aggravated felony convictions. Level 2s—medium-risk detainees—may not include detainees whose most recent conviction was for a severe offense, or detainees with a pattern or history of violent assaults, whether convicted or not. ICE/DRO Detention Standard, "Classification System."

[41] At the time of Human Rights First's tours, detainees took their meals in their housing units—rather than in a separate cafeteria—at Essex County jail, Hudson County jail, Elizabeth Detention Center, Broward Transitional Center, ICA-Farmville, and South Texas Detention Facility.

[42] 2008 Operations Manual ICE Performance Based National Detention Standards (PBNDS), Part 5, Standard 29, "Recreation."

[43] American Civil Liberties Union of Arizona, *In Their Own Words: Enduring Abuse in Arizona Immigration Detention Centers* (Phoenix: ACLU of Arizona, 2011).

[44] 2000 Detention Operations Manual National Detention Standards (NDS), INS Detention Standard, "Recreation," and 2008 Operations Manual ICE Performance Based National Detention Standards (PBNDS), Part 5, Standard 29, "Recreation." The 2000 NDS requires only 5 hours per week of outdoor access, and the 2008 PBNDS requires 7.

[45] For example, the James A. Musick Facility (California) permits four or five hours of outdoor recreation each day. Human Rights First tour, June 14, 2011.

[46] At Mira Loma Detention Center in California, which holds 1,190 detainees, family visiting hours are limited to Saturdays and Sundays from 7am to 3pm. At LaSalle Detention Facility in Louisiana, which holds 998 detainees and is located 230 miles from New Orleans and 140 miles from Baton Rouge, families may visit on Saturdays, Sundays, and holidays, from 8am to 4pm. They are limited to just 30 minutes. Neither facility permits contact visits.

[47] ACLU of Arizona, *In Their Own Words*.

[48] Human Rights First interviews with local service providers, August 2010, March 2011, and September 2011; "Jack Harwell Detention Center," last modified October 4, 2011, accessed October 4, 2011, http://www.cecintl.com/facilities_sf_tx_017.html.

[49] In an informal survey of legal service providers and visitation projects across the country in March and September 2011, as well as our tours in 2010 and 2011, Human Rights First was able to identify only ten detention facilities where contact visits are regularly available to detainees and their families— Elizabeth Detention Center, Hudson County Jail, Monmouth County jail (with advance permission) Port Isabel Detention Center (on special request), Eloy Federal Contract Facility (though visitation space is insufficient for the volume of legal and non-legal visits), T. Don Hutto Residential Detention Center, Berks Family Residential Center, Broward Transitional Center, Karnes County Correctional Center, and ICA Farmville.

[50] See, e.g. National Institute of Corrections, *Inmate Behavior Management: The Key to a Safe and Secure Jail* (Washington, DC: NIC, 2009), p. 15-16 (noting how provision of "structured activities" by jails "contributes to the overall goals of the behavior management plan.").

[51] USCIRF, *Asylum Seekers in Expedited Removal*, p. 189; USCIRF, *Expedited Removal Study Report Card*, p. 5.

[52] ICE, "Fact Sheet: 2009 Immigration Detention Reforms."

[53] 2009 DHS/ICE Report, p. 21.

[54] Ibid. p. 2-3.

[55] See Convention Relating to the Status of Refugees, 189 U.N.T.S. 150, art. 31 (prohibiting states from imposing penalties on those refugees who "present themselves without delay" to the appropriate authorities) (hereinafter cited as Refugee Convention); International Covenant on Civil and Political Rights, 999 U.N.T.S. 171, art. 9 (providing that "[e]veryone has the right to liberty and security of person" and "[n]o one shall be subjected to arbitrary arrest and detention.") (hereinafter cited as ICCPR).

[56] IACHR Report, p. 85.

[57] UN Human Rights Council, *Report of the Special Rapporteur on the Human Rights of Migrants, Jorge Bustamante: Mission to the United States of America*, A/HRC/7/12/Add.2 (March 5, 2008), ¶ 28, available at http://www.unhcr.org/refworld/docid/47d647462.html (hereinafter cited as UNHCR, *Mission to America*).

[58] See 2009 DHS/ICE Report, p. 27; "Fact Sheet: T. Don Hutto Residential Center," last modified October 4, 2011, accessed October 4, 2011, http://www.ice.gov/news/library/factsheets/facilities-hutto.htm

[59] Enforcement and Removal Operations, Immigration and Customs Enforcement, Department of Homeland Security, "ERO Detention Management Division, Authorized Facility List," as of July 18, 2011 and March 14, 2011, provided to NGO-ICE Enforcement Working Group (hereinafter cited as ERO Facility List). ICE holds up to 33,400 immigrant detainees every day.

[60] Natasha Lindstrom, "Geo Group finalizes $28 million purchase of Adelanto prison," *Daily Press*, June 7, 2010, available at http://www.vvdailypress.com/articles/adelanto-19728-prison-purchase.html.

[61] Natasha Lindstrom, "Company plans prison for illegal immigrants: Adelanto facility hinges on winning contract," *Daily Press*, September 22, 2009, available at http://www.allbusiness.com/legal/property-law-real-property-zoning-land-use/13013932-1.html.

[62] David Olson, "First Inland detention center opening," *The Press-Enterprise*, August 29, 2011, available at http://www.pe.com/localnews/stories/PE_News_Local_D_detention29.3ac3dd6.html.

[63] Amy Taxin, "Immigration adds 1,300 beds for California detainees," *San Jose Mercury News*, June 1, 2011, available at http://www.mercurynews.com/ci_18182755?IADID.

[64] Adelanto IGSA.

[65] Richard Khavkine, "Essex County signs new 5-year agreement that could increase number of immigrant detainees, generate $5M annually," *New Jersey Star-Ledger*, August 12, 2011, available at http://www.nj.com/news/index.ssf/2011/08/essex_county_signs_new_5-year.html.

[66] Human Rights First tour of Essex County Correctional Facility on February 24, 2011.

[67] GEO Group, "The GEO Group Signs Contract for the Continued Management of the Aurora ICE Processing Center in Colorado," news release, September 19, 2011.

[68] ICE has indicated that it may want to expand capacity at those facilities to 1,400 in the future. California Environmental Quality Act Analysis, Orange County Proposed Agreement to House Federal Civil Detainees (2010), p. 1 (hereinafter cited as Orange County CEQA Analysis).

[69] Correspondence with senior ICE officials, October 1, 2011.

[70] Lynn Brezosky, "ICE plans pullout from Raymondville," *San Antonio Express-News*, June 10, 2011.

[71] Intergovernmental Service Agreement between the United States Department of Homeland Security, U.S. Immigration and Customs Enforcement, Office of Removal and Enforcement Operations and Essex County, EROIGSA-11-0008, obtained by the New Jersey Advocates for Immigrant Detainees, on file with Human Rights First (hereinafter cited as Essex County IGSA).

[71] ERO Facility List, July 18, 2011.

[72] ERO Facility List, July 18, 2011.

[73] Lynette Curtis, "ICE utilizes new beds in Henderson," *Las Vegas Review-Journal,* February 26, 2011 available at http://www.lvrj.com/news/ice-utilizes-new-beds-in-henderson-116973383.html; see also "Henderson Police—Detention Center," last modified September 27, 2011, http://www.cityofhenderson.com/police/detention.php.

[74] Jeremy Redmon, "ICE to house more suspected illegal immigrants in Georgia," *Atlanta Journal-Constitution*, December 16, 2010, available at http://www.ajc.com/news/georgia-politics-elections/feds-stick-to-their-815204.html; Jeremy Redmon, "Feds stick to their focus as Georgia lawmakers seek to crack down on illegal immigrants," *Atlanta Journal-Constitution,* January 25, 2011, available at http://www.ajc.com/news/georgia-politics-elections/feds-stick-to-their-815204.html.

[75] ERO Facility List, July 18, 2011.

[76] Elias Groll, "O.C. Jail to House Immigration Detainees," *Orange County Register,* July 20, 2010, available at http://www.ocregister.com/articles/immigration-258499-beds-supervisors.html. ERO Facility List, July 18, 2011.

[77] Human Rights First tour of James A. Musick Facility and Theo Lacy on June 14, 2011.

[78] Regina Davis, "A new jail in McLennan County—but no inmates to fill it," *Waco Tribune*, April 23, 2010.

[79] Correspondence with local legal service providers, September 2011.

[80] For detailed data on immigrant detainee transfers and discussion on the hardships they create, see Human Rights Watch, *Locked Up Far Away: The Transfer of Immigrants to Remote Detention Centers in the United States*, (New York: Human Rights Watch, 2009).

[81] 2009 DHS/ICE Report, p. 2-3.

[82] DHS/ICE, *Endgame*, p. 2-12.

[83] ICE bed space has increased from 20,000 in FY 2005 to 33,400 in FY 2012—a 67 percent jump. Congress plays a key role by explicitly authorizing ICE's 33,400 detention beds; the most recent DHS appropriations bill stated that "funding made available under this heading [Immigration and Customs Enforcement] shall maintain a level of *not less than 33,400 detention beds* through September 30, 2010." Cite. ICE has also promised to "support any additional bed space requirements generated by Secure Communities' interoperability program" in FY 11 and FY12, which could bring the total ICE bed space above 33,400. Department of Homeland Security, *Fiscal Year 2012 Congressional Budget Justification*, p. 36, 37. See *FY 2005 Budget Request for the U.S. Immigration and Customs Enforcement, Before the House Appropriations Comm., Subcomm. on Homeland Sec.*, 108th Cong. (March 17, 2004) (testimony of Michael J. Garcia, Assistant Secretary, Immigration and Customs Enforcement), available at http://www.ice.gov/doclib/news/library/speeches/0403GARFY05AppropTesty.pdf; *U.S. Immigration and Customs Enforcement FY 2012 Budget Request, Before the House Appropriations Comm., Subcomm. on Homeland Sec.*, 112th Cong. (March 11, 2011) (testimony of John Morton, Assistant Secretary, Immigration and Customs Enforcement), available at http://www.ice.gov/doclib/news/library/speeches/031111morton.pdf; Department of Homeland Security Appropriations Act 2010, Public Law 111-83, 111th Cong., 1st sess. (October 28, 2009).

[84] OIS, *Immigration Enforcement Actions: 2010*, p. 1; Office of Immigration Statistics—Policy Directorate, Department of Homeland Security, *Immigration Enforcement Actions: 2005*, (Washington, DC: DHS, 2006).

[85] In FY 2005, ICE's enacted and supplemental budget for Detention and Removal Operations, Custody Operations was $864,125,000. See ICE, *Fact Sheet—Fiscal Year 2005*, available at http://www.ice.gov/doclib/news/library/factsheets/pdf/2005budgetfactsheet.pdf.

[86] Department of Homeland Security, *Fiscal Year 2012 Congressional Budget Justification, U.S. Immigration and Customs Enforcement, Salaries and Expenses, Custody & Operations*, p. 57. The daily cost of $122 includes costs of beds, healthcare, guard contracts, facility costs, and administrative overhead.

[87] ICE, *Report to Congress: Detained Asylum Seekers Fiscal Year 2008* (2009); 2009 DHS/ICE Report, p. 6.

[88] DHS/ICE, *Detention and Removal Operations Report Required by Section 903 of the Haitian Refugee Immigration Fairness Act (PL-105-277), Detained Asylum Seekers Fiscal Year 2008* (Washington, DC: DHS, 2009). Based on the data provided in this Section 903 report, Human Rights First calculated that the average length of stay for detained asylum seekers—including affirmative asylum seekers, asylum seekers who passed credible fear interviews, and defensive asylum seekers—was 102.4 days in fiscal year 2008. 153 detained asylum seekers were held for a year or longer that year. ICE has not yet produced the equivalent data for fiscal years 2009 or 2010, despite a requirement from Congress that the agency do so, and despite regular inquiries from Human Rights First since 2009 for this data.

[89] Supra, note 86.

[90] ICE, "Fact Sheet: ICE Detention Reform Principles;" see also DHS, "Secretary Napolitano and ICE Assistant Secretary Morton announce new immigration detention reform initiatives," news release, October 6, 2009 ("Each of the reforms announced today are expected to be budget neutral or result in cost savings through reduced reliance on contractors to perform key federal duties and additional oversight of all contracts.").

[91] DHS press conference, October 6, 2009.

[92] Publicly quoted costs for ATDs vary. DHS's FY 2009 nationwide ATD plan reported that ATDs cost $8.88 per day. DHS/ICE, "Report to Congress: Alternatives to Detention Nationwide Program Implementation," April 1, 2010, note 4. At a conference held by the Migration Policy Institute, former ICE Assistant Secretary Julie Myers Wood (who served under President George W. Bush) said that the average daily cost of ATDs was $6.84. Migration Policy Institute, "Plenary Session III: Detention Reform—Standards, Alternatives, and Vulnerable Populations," *8th Annual Immigration Law & Policy Conference*, April 26, 2011.

[93] BI and ICE have named the full-service and technology-only programs together "ISAP II"—a new version of the Intensive Supervision Appearance Program that began as a pilot in 2004. BI Incorporated, *Intensive Supervision Appearance Program II: An Alternatives to Detention Program for the U.S. Department of Homeland Security*, (BI Incorporated, CY 2010), p. 4, 5, 17, 21.

[94] Human Rights First, *U.S. Detention of Asylum Seekers: Seeking Protection, Finding Prison*, (New York: Human Rights First, 2009), p. 63-67; Lutheran Immigration and Refugee Service, *Unlocking Liberty: Increasing the Use of Community Support Programs as Alternatives to Immigration Detention in the United States*, (Baltimore: Lutheran Immigration and Refugee Service, forthcoming).

[95] Department of Homeland Security, *Fiscal Year 2012 Congressional Budget Justification*, p. 59. Check..

[96] 2009 DHS/ICE Report, p. 2-3.

[97] DHS press conference, October 6, 2009.

[98] Human Rights First interview with Jeanne Woodford, former Secretary of the California Department of Corrections and former warden of San Quentin State Prison, March 22, 2011.

[99] DHS/ICE, *Endgame*, p. 2-12.

[100] 2009 DHS/ICE Report, p. 4.

[101] ICE, "Fact Sheet: 2009 Immigration Detention Reforms."

[102] Supra, note 19.

[103] Morton, MPI Speakers Series.

[104] ICE, "Fact Sheet: ICE Detention Reform Principles."

[105] *Department of Homeland Security Oversight, Before the Senate Comm. on the Judiciary*, 112th Cong. (March 9, 2011) (testimony of Janet Napolitano, Secretary, Department of Homeland Security), available at http://www.dhs.gov/ynews/testimony/testimony_1299683039975.shtm.

[106] Schriro testimony, *Preliminary Assessment*.

[107] See "FAQ," American Correctional Association, last modified September 28, 2011, accessed September 28, 2011, https://www.aca.org/standards/faq.asp#overview_benefits.

[108] *INS Hopes to Bring Uniformity to Detention Facilities' Processes with Release of Comprehensive Standards*, 77 NO. 45 Interpreter Releases 1637 (2000).

[109] Human Rights First tour of El Centro Service Processing Center, June 16, 2011.

[110] Human Rights First tour of Port Isabel Service Processing Center, December 6, 2010.

[111] ICE has undertaken the project of revising the 2008 PBNDS (The draft "PBNDS 2010" were leaked to a reporter at the Houston Chronicle in September 2010 and posted here: http://www.scribd.com/doc/38412265/Performance-Based-National-Detention-Standard-2010.) However, the revised PBNDS have yet to be released or rolled out to facilities, despite ICE's promise to do so at facilities holding 55 percent of its detainees by the end of 2010, and 85 percent by the end of 2011. ICE's commitment to rolling out the revised PBNDS is detailed on its own web site at "Detention Reform Accomplishments," last modified September 28, 2011, accessed September 28, 2011, http://www.ice.gov/detention-reform/detention-reform.htm. In 2011, ICE characterized the revised PBNDS to Congress as "reflect[ing] ICE's civil detention mission"—despite the fact that they remain explicitly based on American Correctional Association standards. Department of Homeland Security, *Fiscal Year 2012 Congressional Budget Justification*, p. 34: "DRO and ICE's Office of Detention Policy and Planning (ODPP) are in the final stages of modernizing ICE's detention standards. In collaboration with various stakeholders, ICE has drafted the 2010 Performance-Based National Detention Standards (PBNDS), which focus on the outcomes that the required procedures are expected to accomplish. These new standards will reflect ICE's civil detention mission and create a new detention system geared to the unique needs of those in ICE custody."

[112] 2009 DHS/ICE Report, p. 2. Just two ICE-authorized facilities are inspected against other standards—T. Don Hutto Residential Detention Center (Taylor, TX) and Berks Family Residential Center (Leesport, PA).

[113] USCIRF, *Asylum Seekers in Expedited Removal*, p. 181

[114] Morton, MPI Speakers Series.

[115] 2009 DHS/ICE Report, p. 19..

[116] ICE has created at least two different versions of this SOO. The Texas SOO, which led to ICE's agreement with Karnes County and GEO Group, contained no reference to standards. The Florida SOO and the Chicago SOO, which led to ICE's tentative choice to partner with CCA in both cases, and the Northeast SOO, which led to a contract with Essex County, New Jersey, all indicate an expectation that the new facilities' "secure" beds (80 percent of the beds) will comply with the optimum performance levels of the existing PBNDS (or pending PBNDS 2010), and its "non-secure" beds (20 percent of the beds) will comply with Adult Residential Standards, "currently under development."

[117] INS, *2000 Detention Operations Manual National Detention Standards (NDS), INS Detention Standards*, "Detainee Classification System," "Recreation," and "Visitation." ICE, *2008 Operations Manual ICE Performance Based National Detention Standards (PBNDS)*, Part 2, Standard 5, "Classification System"; Part 5, Standard 29, "Recreation"; and Part 5, Standard 32, "Visitation."

[118] Intergovernmental Service Agreement between DHS/ICE and Karnes County, EROIGSA-11-0004, December 7, 2010 (hereinafter cited as Karnes County IGSA), obtained by Grassroots Leadership through an open records request to Karnes County, on file with Human Rights First.

[119] See DHS/ICE, "Statement of Objectives, Immigration Detention Reform, Request for Inter-governmental Service Agreement (IGSA) Concept Proposal."

[120] See Essex County IGSA; Karnes County IGSA; Inter-Governmental Service Agreement between the DHS/ICE Office of Enforcement and Removal Operations and County of Orange, DROIGSA-10-0001, dated July 6, 2010. Available from Orange County Board of Supervisors (Hereinafter cited as Orange County IGSA). ICE's new contract with Essex County for the operation of Delaney Hall and Essex County jail states: "The parties to this IGSA agree to enter into negotiations if and when the ICE Detention Standards are updated. This Agreement will be modified in writing upon mutual agreement." If "updated" could refer to the development of new standards not based on ACA standards, then this contract does mention the potential for new standards. The contract with Essex County—which is over 200 pages long—also incorporates a Performance Work Statement for Delaney Hall, as an attachment, which requires in a single location compliance with the Civil Detention Statement of Objectives, which is included as a separate attachment. Essex County IGSA.

[121] Human Rights First correspondence with senior ICE officials, October 1, 2011.

[122] Jane Holl Lute, DHS Deputy Secretary, letter to Michael Wishnie, Yale Law School and Paromita Shah, National Immigration Project of the National Lawyers Guild, July 24, 2009, available at http://clearinghouse.net/chDocs/public/IM-NY-0045-0004.pdf.

[123] ICE, "ICE announces new Performance-Based National Detention Standards for all ICE detention facilities," news release, September 12, 2008, available at http://www.ice.gov/news/releases/0809/080912washington.htm..

[124] DHS/ICE, *Endgame*, 2-3 and 2-4.

[125] Dora Schriro, "Improving Conditions of Confinement for Criminal Inmates and Immigrant Detainees," *American Criminal Law Review*, vol. 47, no. 4, (2010), p. 1442. ("The operation of institutions detaining immigrants for ICE would be measurably improved by adopting standards that sustain the infrastructure for constitutional compliance."); Randall Atlas, "Changes in Prison Facilities as a Function of Correctional Philosophy," in *History of Prisons*, Chapter 3, ed. Roger Dunham (1991). (Discussing the development of corrections standards in the 1960s and 1970s, he writes that the standards "are used as a basis for auditing and determining whether applicant and candidate facilities meet established minimum requirements and should be certified or accredited"—a basis that was previously lacking.)

[126] Malcolm M. Feeley and Van Swearingen, *The Prison Conditions Cases and the Bureaucratization of American Corrections: Influences, Impacts and Implications*, 24 Pace L. Rev. 433 (2004) ("[S]tandards were developed by professional organizations and promulgated into the regulations in the most highly regarded prison systems.")

[127] CQ Newsmaker Transcripts, "Immigration and Customs Enforcement Assistant Secretary John Morton Holds Conference Call."

[128] For an analysis of the capacity of ICE's existing data systems and recommendations for improvement, see Migration Policy Institute, *Immigrant Detention: Can ICE Meet Its Legal Imperatives and Case Management Responsibilities?* (Washington, DC: MPI, 2009), particularly pp. 32-34 in relation to standards compliance, available at http://www.migrationpolicy.org/pubs/detentionreportSept1009.pdf.

[129] Human Rights First correspondence with senior ICE officials, October 1, 2011

[130] Village of Crete, "A White Paper Presented by the Village of Crete, Illinois and CCA in Response to Immigration and Customs Enforcement Request for Inter-Governmental Service Agreement (IGSA) Concept Proposal: Chicago," redacted, November 15, 2010; Matt Marshman, ICE Contracting Officer, letter to Michael Einhorn, Crete Village President, June 27, 2011. Both documents obtained by Human Rights First through Illinois Freedom of Information Act request.

[131] Khavkine, "Essex County signs new 5-year agreement.".

[132] Human Rights First tours of Delaney Hall, February 24, 2011, and July 26, 2011.

[133] Human Rights First correspondence with visitation volunteer from IRATE/First Friends, October 5, 2011.

[134] On the day of our February 24th tour, the smell was so intensely bad that ICE and county officials had to cover their faces with jackets while running from their cars into Delaney Hall to meet us. The Ironbound, where the Essex County jail and Delaney Hall are located, is one of the nation's most polluted neighborhoods. It is home to the biggest Superfund site in the country (where 18 miles of the Passaic River is contaminated with dioxin), the largest garbage incinerator in New Jersey, and many other polluted or polluting sites from both past and present industries. Over 8 million tons of toxic emissions are produced there annually. Human Rights First interview with Cynthia Mellon, Ironbound Community Corporation, April 21, 2011.

[135] GEO Group, "The GEO Group Announces Contract for New 600-Bed Immigration Civil Detention Center in Texas," news release, December 8, 2010; Michael Barajas, "Prisons for profit: Deaths, lawsuits don't stop expansion of Geo immigration prisons," *San Antonio Current,* February 14, 2011; Jason Buch, "New detention center in Karnes County," *San Antonio Express News,* December 9, 2010.

[136] Karnes County IGSA, Attachment 1.

[137] The provision states: "Subject to the security needs of the facility, detainees may be allowed to access the courtyard recreation area within the facility's secure perimeter at various hours of the day and early evening."

[138] The provision states: "Under very controlled access, detainees may be allowed internet access in order to contact and maintain family ties."

[139] Groll, "O.C. Jail to House Immigration Detainees;" ERO Facility List," July 18, 2011.

[140] Orange County IGSA

[141] Alfonso Chardy, "ICE picks Southwest Ranches for possible immigration detention center," *Miami Herald*, June 24, 2011, available at http://www.miamiherald.com/2011/06/24/2282834/ice-picks-southwest-ranches-for.html; Roshan Nebhrajani, "One of the nation's largest immigration centers may be built at Southwest Ranches," *Miami Herald*, July 22, 2011, available at http://www.miamiherald.com/2011/07/22/2326928/one-of-the-nations-largest-immigrant.html#ixzz1T3XmUdN1.

[142] Human Rights First correspondence with senior ICE officials, October 1, 2011.

[143] Town of Southwest Ranches, "Immigration Detention Reform: A White Paper Presented by the Town of Southwest Ranches, FL, and CCA in Response to Immigration and Customs Enforcement Request for Inter-Governmental Service Agreement (IGSA) Concept Proposal: Miami," November 15, 2010.

[144] Kirk Semple, "Plan to upgrade New Jersey jail into model for immigration detention centers," *New York Times*, January 28, 2011 ("Federal officials say the county's proposal, which they have tentatively approved, would provide a less penal setting for [immigration] detainees, with improved medical care, amenities and federal oversight — the template for a new kind of detention center they intend to create around the country by renovating existing centers, building new ones and closing others.").

[145] Lynn Brezosky, "ICE plans pullout from Raymondville," *San Antonio Express-News*, June 10, 2011.

[146] . Under Article 31 of the Refugee Convention, refugees should not be penalized for their illegal entry if they present themselves without delay and show good cause for their illegal entry. For asylum seekers and refugees, detention can amount to a penalty when, for example, asylum seekers are deprived of liberty for the mere reason of illegal entry or when detention fails the necessity test under Article 31(2) of the Refugee Convention. See Alice Edwards— UNCHR Expert Consultant, *Back to Basics: The Right to Liberty and Security of Person and 'Alternatives to Detention' of Refugees, Asylum-Seekers, Stateless Persons, and Other Migrants* (Geneva: UNHCR, 2011), PPLA/2011/01.Rev.1, p. 11, n. 64; see also Noll, 'Article 31(Refugees lawfully in the country of refuge),' in A. Zimmermann (ed.), *Commentary on the 1951 Convention relating to the Status of Refugees* (Oxford: Oxford University Press, 2011), p. 1243, ¶ 96.

[147] Email survey of legal service providers, March and September 2011.

[148] Human Rights First tour on December 10, 2010.

[149] Human Rights First tour on December 6, 2010.

[150] Susan Carroll, "ICE to make detention centers more humane," *Houston Chronicle*, June 8, 2010, available at http://www.chron.com/disp/story.mpl/special/immigration/7043040.html (accessed September 28, 2011); leaked email from Steven Conry, Vice President, Corrections Corporation of America, May 27, 2010. CCA's nine facilities include North Georgia Detention Center, Elizabeth Detention Center (New Jersey), Laredo Processing Center (Texas), Stewart Detention Center (Georgia), Eloy Federal Contract Facility (Arizona), Florence Correctional Center (Arizona), Houston Contract Detention Facility (Texas), San Diego Correctional Facility (California), and T. Don Hutto Residential Detention Center (Texas). CCA also operates some jails that hold ICE detainees under IGSAs, including Central Arizona Detention Center (Arizona), Western Tennessee Detention Facility, Metro/Davidson County Detention Facility (Tennessee), and Torrance County Detention Center (New Mexico).

[151] Information based on interviews with local legal service providers working at each facility, September 2011.

[152] See, e.g. ICE, "Fact Sheet: ICE Detention Reform Principles and Next Steps."

[153] See, e.g., A.E. Bottoms, "Interpersonal Violence and Social Order in Prison," in *Crime and Justice: A Review of Research*, vol. 26, eds. M. Tonry & J. Petersilia (1999), p. 243, n. 32.

[154] ICE Council 118 of the American Federation of Government Employees, "ICE union vote of no confidence," news release, July 23, 2010.

[155] *Moving Toward More Effective Immigration Detention Management*, Before the House Homeland Sec. Comm., Subcomm. on Border, Maritime, and Global Counterterrorism, 111th Cong. (December 10, 2009) (statement by Christopher L. Crane, Detention and Removal Operations, American Federation of Government Employees National ICE Council-118).

[156] Lorenzo Garza, Executive Vice President, AFGE Council 118 ICE, "Reforms to ICE's Detention System E-Mail," *AFGE Local 207 Blog*, September 30, 2009, available at http://www.afgelocal207.com/From-Council-118.html.

[157] Memorandum from ICE Field Office Director Advisory Committee to John Morton, ICE Assistant Secretary, "Response to 'Immigration Detention Overview and Recommendations,'" undated, available at http://centerforinvestigativereporting.org/files/documents/ICEmemo.html.

[158] Supra, notes 27 and 29.

[159] Human Rights First interview, April 1, 2011.

[160] A national bipartisan commission created to examine violence in the U.S. prison and jail systems and make recommendations to improve safety for prisoners, staff, and the public stated in its 2006 report that "few conditions compromise safety more than idleness." The Commission on Safety and Abuse in America's Prisons, *Confronting Confinement*, (New York: Vera Institute of Justice, 2006), p. 12, available at http://www.prisoncommission.org/pdfs/Confronting_Confinement.pdf. Steve J. Martin told Human Rights First that "there is nothing better than programming" to create a safe environment for detainees. Human Rights First interview, April 1, 2011.

[161] "CQ Newsmaker Transcripts, "Immigration and Customs Enforcement Assistant Secretary John Morton Holds Conference Call." ("If we do this right, we will see that our facilities move to a much more sophisticated design and location where we have a certain level of restrictive settings and circumstances for

people who pose a danger to others and to themselves, and less restrictive settings for those people who are simply a risk of flight and need to be detained, but are not otherwise a danger to people.")

162 DHS/ICE, "Statement of Objectives," p. 3.

163 For example, Michele Deitch (criminal justice and juvenile justice expert, University of Texas Law School and LBJ School of Public Affairs) told Human Rights First that "criminal history of detainees should not affect the conditions inside the facility; it could be a risk factor, but far more determinative of custody classification would be the person's institutional behavior." (April 15, 2011)

164 Town of Southwest Ranches, "Immigration Detention Reform;" Village of Crete, "A White Paper;" and "Statement of Objectives, Immigration Detention Reform, Request for Inter-governmental Service Agreement (IGSA) Concept Proposal: North East."

165 Human Rights First interview with Michele Deitch, April 15, 2011.

166 Texas Coalition of Civil and Immigrants Rights Organizations letter to Janet Napolitano, Secretary, Department of Homeland Security, February 24, 2011.

167 Andrea Black, "ICE, Obama cannot build their way out of detention crisis," *New American Media,* March 13, 2011, available at http://newamericamedia.org/2011/03/ice-obama-cannot-build-their-way-out-of-detention-crisis.php; Michael Barajas, "Groups urge DHS to end new prison contract with GEO," *San Antonio Current,* February 24, 2011, available at http://blogs.sacurrent.com/?p=5574; "The Influence of the Private Prison Industry in Immigration Detention," Detention Watch Network, May 11, 2011, http://www.detentionwatchnetwork.org/privateprisons.

168 Barajas, "Prisons for Profit."

169 Sam Dolnick, " Political Links Seen Behind New Jersey Detention Center Bid," *New York Times*, July 28, 2011, available at http://www.nytimes.com/2011/07/28/nyregion/political-links-seen-behind-essex-county-detention-center-bid.htm.

170 Elizabeth Summers, "ICE facility to stay in Etowah County," *The Sand Mountain Reporter*, April 8, 2011, available at http://www.sandmountainreporter.com/news/local/article_57739968-6221-11e0-ab59-001cc4c002e0.html.

171 Supra, note 18.

172 ICE, "Fact Sheet: 2009 Immigration Detention Reforms."

173 See "Detention Reform Accomplishments," as well as DHS, *Fiscal Year 2012 Congressional Budget Justification*.

174 "ICE Health Service Corps Provider Information," ICE Health Service Corps, last modified January 11, 2010, http://www.icehealth.org/ManagedCare/Providers.shtm; ICE Health Service Corps, *Detainee Covered Services* (Washington, DC: DHS/ICE, 2010), available at http://www.icehealth.org/ManagedCare/IHSC%202010%20Detainee%20Covered%20Service%20Package_12-28-10.pdf; ACLU of San Diego, "Practice Advisory: Health Care for ICE Detainees after the *Woods v. Morton* Settlement," available at http://www.aclusandiego.org/article_downloads/001165/Woods%20Practice%20Advisory.pdf.

175 In 2009, according to ICE data on file with Human Rights First, the release rate was 71 percent. In 2010, it was 67 percent, and in the first six months of 2011, it was 80 percent.

176 See Memorandum by John Morton, ICE Director, to All Field Office Directors, All Special Agents in Charge, and All Chief Counsel, "Exercising Prosecutorial Discretion Consistent with the Civil Immigration Enforcement Priorities of the Agency for the Apprehension, Detention, and Removal of Aliens," June 17, 2011, available at http://www.ice.gov/doclib/secure-communities/pdf/prosecutorial-discretion-memo.pdf.

177 Cecilia Muñoz, "Immigration Update: Maximizing Public Safety and Better Focusing Resources," *The White House Blog*, August 18, 2011, available at http://www.whitehouse.gov/blog/2011/08/18/immigration-update-maximizing-public-safety-and-better-focusing-resources.

178 ACLU of Arizona, *In Their Own Words*.

179 ACLU of New Mexico, Regional Center for Border Rights, *Outsourcing Responsibility: The Human Cost of Privatized Immigration Detention in Otero County* (Las Cruces: ACLU of New Mexico, Regional Center for Border Rights, 2011), available at http://aclu-nm.org/wp-content/uploads/2011/01/OCPC-Report.pdf.

180 Heartland Alliance, National Immigrant Justice Center, "Mass Civil Rights Complaint Details Systemic Abuse of Sexual Minorities in US Immigration Detention," April 13, 2011, available at http://www.immigrantjustice.org/press_releases/mass-civil-rights-complaint-details-systemic-abuse-sexual-minorities-us-immigration-d. For further accounts of ongoing concerns with the immigration detention system, see National Immigrant Justice Center/Detention Watch Network/Midwest Coalition for Human Rights, *Year One Report Card: Human Rights and the Obama Administration's Immigration Detention Reforms* (Chicago: NIJC/DWN/MCHR, 2010), available at http://www.immigrantjustice.org/icereportcard.

181 IACHR Report, ¶ 275-96, p. 97-107.

182 DHS Office of the Inspector General, *Management of Mental Health Cases*.

183 National Prison Rape Elimination Commission, *National Prison Rape Elimination Commission Report* (Washington, DC: 2009), ch. 9, available at https://www.ncjrs.gov/pdffiles1/226680.pdf.

184 In response, a group of 11 national nongovernmental organizations wrote in a February 15, 2011, letter to President Barack Obama to urge that immigration detention facilities be covered under PREA: "The exclusion of immigration detention from standards on preventing, detecting, and responding to sexual assault in custody is unjustifiable. It ignores the history of sexual assault in immigration detention, is inconsistent with the intent of PREA and the

administration's own efforts at detention reform, and implicates basic human rights obligations undertaken by the United States." Nationwide coalition of 11 human rights NGOs, letter to Barack Obama, President, United States of America, February 15, 2011, available at http://www.hrw.org/node/96407.

[185] Human Rights First, *U.S. Detention of Asylum Seekers,* p. 32-33.

[186] See INA § 236(c); 8 CFR § 208.30, 212.5, 235.3, and 1003.19.

[187] Provisions located mainly at 8 CFR § 1003.19 and § 212.5, as well as at § 208.30 and § 235.3

[188] ICCPR, art. 9(4).

[189] While asylum seekers have occasionally tried to file federal court habeas petitions to challenge parole denials, these petitions do not serve as an effective mechanism for asylum seekers to obtain a timely and independent review of ICE decisions to deny them parole. Practically speaking, it can take months or longer before a decision is issued in these cases. Some federal courts have refused to review parole denials for asylum seekers, in some cases citing a lack of jurisdiction and in other cases emphasizing that they are obligated to defer to the judgment of immigration officials as long as a reason was given for the parole denial. See e.g. *Nadarajah v Gonzalez*, 443 F.3d 1069, 1075 (9th Cir. 2006) (if a "facially legitimate and bona fide" reason for denying parole is provided, the "denial of parole is essentially unreviewable." Finding agency abused its discretion in denying parole because the reasons it provided were not facially legitimate and bona fide). See also *Veerikathy v INS*, 98 Civ. 2591, 1998 U.S. Dist. LEXIS 19360 (E.D.N.Y. Oct. 9, 1998); *Zhang v. Slattery*, 840 F. Supp. 292 (S.D.N.Y. 1994); see also *Bertrand v. Sava*, 684 F.2d 204 (2d Cir. 1982).

[190] Petitions on file with Human Rights First.

[191] Every member State of the United Nations undergoes this review every four years. See Human Rights First, *Human Rights First Submission to the Office of the High Commissioner for Human Rights, Universal Periodic Review: United States of America* (New York: Human Rights First, 2010), p. 5, available at http://www.humanrightsfirst.org/wp-content/uploads/pdf/HRF_UPR_Submission_HRC_April_2010.pdf; and The Advocates for Human Rights, *United States of America, Submission to the United Nations Universal Periodic Review: Migrants, Refugees, and Asylum Seekers* (Minneapolis: The Advocates for Human Rights, 2010) submitted by 18 national and 30 state and local groups, including Human Rights First, p. 5, ¶ 8, and p. 13, ¶ 46, available at http://www.humanrightsfirst.org/wp-content/uploads/pdf/Cluster_Submission_Refugees_Migrants.pdf.

[192] Janet Napolitano, DHS Secretary, letter to Mary Meg McCarthy, NIJC Executive Diretcor, "re: Petition for Rulemaking to Create Presumption of Parole for Arriving Asylum Seekers Who Pass a Credible Fear Interview, March 15, 2010," December 10, 2010, p. 4, on file with Human Rights First..

[193] "United States of America, Submission to the United Nations Universal Periodic Review: Migrants, Refugees, and Asylum Seekers," submitted by 18 national and 30 state and local groups, including Human Rights First, p. 5, ¶ 8, at http://www.humanrightsfirst.org/wp-content/uploads/pdf/Cluster_Submission_Refugees_Migrants.pdf; and "United States of America, Submission to the United National Universal Periodic Review: Human Rights Violations in the Immigrant Detention System," submitted by 15 contributing stakeholders and 11 endorsers, p. 8, on file with Human Rights First. See also Amnesty International, "Jailed Without Justice: Immigration Detention in the USA," March 2009, p. 44.

[194] Supra, note 92.

[195] Human Rights First calculation, based on ICE's projected daily detention cost of $122.

[196] Lutheran Immigration and Refugee Service, *Unlocking Liberty* (forthcoming) ("The case management described by ICE [in the full-service program], however, does not rise to the level of intensive, ongoing coordination of referrals to community-based services that defines traditional case management service delivery models.")

[197] BI and ICE have named the full-service and technology-only programs together "ISAP II"—a new version of the Intensive Supervision Appearance Program that began as a pilot in 2004. BI Incorporated, *Intensive Supervision*, p. 4, 5, 17, 21.

[198] Human Rights First, *U.S. Detention of Asylum Seekers,* notes 144 and 152.

[199] Edwards, *Back to Basics*, p. iii.

[200] *C v. Australia,* Human Rights Committee, 76th Session, Comm. No. 900/1999, U.N. Doc. CCPR/C/76/D/900/1999 (Oct. 28, 2002), ¶ 8.2 (asylum seeker's detention arbitrary within meaning of ICCPR where State party had "not demonstrated that, in the light of the author's particular circumstances, there were not less invasive means of achieving the same ends" such as reporting requirements or sureties); see also Eleanor Acer and Jake Goodman, *Reaffirming Rights: Human Rights Protections of Migrants, Asylum Seekers, and Refugees in Immigration Detention*, 24 Geo. Immigr. L.J. 507, 516.

[201] ICCPR, art. 9(4) (emphasis added); See UN General Assembly Resolution, *Body of Principles for the Protection of All Persons under Any Form of Detention or Imprisonment*, Principle 11, A/RES/43/173, (Dec. 9, 1988), available at http://www.unhcr.org/refworld/docid/3b00f219c.html (hereinafter cited as UN Body of Principles).

[202] *Torres v. Finland*, UN GAOR, 45th Sess., Supp. No. 40, UN Doc. A/45/40 (1990), ¶ 7.2 (Article 9, ¶ 4, "envisages that the legality of detention will be determined by a court so as to ensure a higher degree of objectivity and independence..."); see Acer and Goodman, *Reaffirming Rights*, p. 518-24.

[203] See e.g. *A v. Australia*, U.N. Human Rights Comm. Communication No. 560/1993, U.N. Doc. CCPR/C/59/D/560/1993 (Apr. 30, 1997), ¶ 9.5, (stating "what is decisive for the purposes of article 9, ¶ 4, is that such review is, in its effects, real and not merely formal."); see also Acer and Goodman, *Reaffirming Rights*, p. 519-20.

[204] UNHCR, UNHCR's Revised Guidelines, Guideline 5(iii).

[205] UNHCR, *Mission to the United States of America*, ¶ 122-23; IACHR Report, ¶ 139, 418, 529, 431.

[206] Under Article 31 of the Refugee Convention, refugees should not be penalized for their illegal entry if they present themselves without delay and show good cause for their illegal entry. For asylum seekers and refugees, detention can amount to a penalty when, for example, asylum seekers are deprived of liberty for the mere reason of illegal entry or when detention fails the necessity test under Article 31(2) of the Refugee Convention. See Edwards, *Back to Basics*, p. 11, n. 64; see also Noll, 'Article 31(Refugees lawfully in the country of refuge),' p. 1243, ¶ 96.

[207] The actual amount would depend on the average length of time that an individual remains in an ATD program as well as the total number of individuals enrolled in ATDs. $88 million would cover 17,000 individuals enrolled in ATDs for an average of 180 days; $513 million would cover 100,000 individuals for an average of 310 days, the current average length of supervision. According to the plan, a reduction of the average length of supervision would require EOIR to place ATD cases on the detained docket, on an expedited schedule, rather than on the non-detained docket, as is current practice—which would require additional funding for EOIR.

[208] As discussed in a comprehensive legal study issued by UNHCR in 2011, measures that are labeled "alternatives to detention" can sometimes constitute alternative forms of detention, and some courts have recognized that the use of ankle monitors can amount to custody. Edwards, *Back to Basics*, p. 9, n. 55. (citing various U.S. cases, some concluding ankle monitor did not constitute custody, but also citing 2008 case that found that ankle monitor and related restrictions amounted to custody); see also Executive Office for Immigration Review, Immigration Court, Los Angeles, USA, May 18, 2008, 18 May 2008, parties are not named, before Bass L.J., available at: http://www.bibdaily.com/pdfs/Bass%20IJ%205-18-08%20electronic%20bracelet%20bond%20decision.pdf.

[209] *Confirmation Hearing, Before the Senate Comm. On Homeland Sec. and Gov. Affairs* (July 26, 2007) (pre-hearing questionnaire of Julie Myers, ICE Assistant Secretary).

[210] DHS, *FY 2012 Congressional Budget Justification*, p. 43, 59.

[211] Human Rights First, *U.S. Detention of Asylum Seekers*, p. 63-67; Lutheran Immigration and Refugee Service, *Unlocking Liberty* (forthcoming(; Vera Institute of Justice, *Testing Community Supervision for the INS: An Evaluation of the Appearance Assistance Program–Volume 1* (New York: Vera Institute of Justice, 2000), p. ii, iii.

[212] Edwards, *Back to Basics*, p. 84; and International Detention Coalition, *There Are Alternatives: A Handbook for Preventing Unnecessary Immigration Detention* (Melbourne: International Detention Coalition, 2011), p. 7-9.

[213] Human Rights First calculations based on ICE's stated average costs of $122 per day for detention and $8.88 for Alternatives to Detention.

[214] Human Rights First correspondence with senior ICE officials, October 1, 2011.

[215] 2009 DHS/ICE Report, p. 17, 20.

[216] Jim Austin and Patricia L. Hardyman, *Objective Prison Classification: A Guide for Correctional Agencies* (Washington, DC: DOJ—National Institute of Corrections, 2004), available at http://www.jfa-associates.com/publications/pcras/06_ObjClass2004.pdf.

[217] Human Rights First, *U.S. Detention of Asylum Seekers*, p. 55-62.

[218] American Bar Association, *Reforming the Immigration System: Proposals to Promote Independence, Fairness, Efficiency and Professionalism in the Adjudication of Removal Cases* (Chicago: American Bar Association, 2000), p. ES-7. In its 2010 Statistical Yearbook the Executive Office for Immigration Review (EOIR) reported that in FY 2010, 43 percent of immigrants in proceedings—both detained and non-detained—were represented by counsel.

[219] Government Accountability Office, *U.S. Asylum System: Significant Variation Existed in Asylum Outcomes Across Immigration Courts and Judges*, GAO-8-940 (Washington, DC: GAO, 2008), p. 30. See also Jaya Ramji-Nogales, Andrew I. Schoenholtz, and Philip G. Schrag, *Refugee Roulette: Disparities in Asylum Adjudication*, 60 Stan. L. Rev. 295 (2007).

[220] DOJ/EOIR, *FY 2010 Statistical Year Book* (Washington, DC: Office of Planning, Analysis, & Technology, 2011), p. G-1, available at http://www.justice.gov/eoir/statspub/fy10syb.pdf; and Charles H. Kuck, *Legal Assistance for Asylum Seekers in Expedited Removal: A Survey of Alternative Practices*, p. 8, in USCIRF, *Asylum Seekers in Expedited Removal*, available at http://www.uscirf.gov/images/stories/pdf/asylum_seekers/legalAssist.pdf. The full quote read: "All judges prefer represented to non-represented cases. Non-represented cases are more difficult to conduct. They require far more effort on the part of the judge. Judges struggle with the alien's difficulties in completing the I-589 (Application for Asylum) in a language they may not be familiar with. The skeletal information provided by the alien must be expanded on by the judge, while maintaining impartiality."

[221] For more information about the Vera Legal Orientation Program, see Legal Orientation Program, Vera Institute of Justice, http://www.vera.org/project/legal-orientation-program.

[222] See Vera Institute of Justice, "Legal Orientation Program: Evaluation and Performance and Outcome Measurement Report, Phase II," May 2008, at http://www.vera.org/download?file=1778/LOP%2Bevalution_updated%2B5-20-08.pdf. List of further support for LOP from nongovernmental organizations, members of Congress, Judge Robert Katzmann of the 2nd Circuit, and Attorney General Eric Holder is on file with Human Rights First.

[223] U.S. Department of Justice FY 2012 Budget at a Glance, Administrative Review and Appeals Executive Office for Immigration Review (EOIR), available at http://www.justice.gov/jmd/2012summary/pdf/fy12-eoir-bud-summary.pdf.

[224] USCIRF, *Asylum Seekers in Expedited Removal*, p. 240.

[225] NIJC surveyed 150 of the estimated 300 immigration detention facilities in operation between August and December 2009, accounting for 31,355 detainee beds out of 32,000 total ICE beds. National Immigrant Justice Center, *Isolated in Detention: Limited Access to Legal Counsel in Immigration*

Detention Facilities Jeopardizes a Fair Day in Court (Chicago: National Immigration Justice Center, 2010), p. 4, 8, available at http://www.immigrantjustice.org/policy-resources/isolatedindetention/intro.html. In May 2008, the Vera Institute of Justice found that "[a]t several sites, the remote location of the detention facilities...a shortage of mentors for legal representatives without experience in immigration law, and a lack of pro bono counsel have all presented significant obstacles" to coordinating pro bono representation for detainees. Vera Institute of Justice, *Legal Orientation Program: Evaluation and Performance Outcome Measurement Report* (New York: Vera Institute of Justice, 2008), p. 24, available at http://www.vera.org/download?file=1778/LOP%2Bevalution_updated%2B5-20-08.pdf.

[226] Based on list of ICE-authorized detention facilities as of 3/14/11. The U.S. Census Bureau reports that there are 76 cities in the country with populations over 250,000. We counted the number of facilities used by ICE as of 3/14/11 located within 60 miles of one of these 76 cities, and then calculated the total number of ICE beds within those parameters. A pro bono or nonprofit attorney based in one of these cities thus dedicates at least two hours—probably much more - out of an eight- to twelve-work hour day, to travel to a detention facility to meet with his or her client for 15 minutes.

[227] Human Rights First, *U.S. Detention of Asylum Seekers*, p. 55.

[228] For a full description of concerns about the use of video-conferencing, see Human Rights First, *U.S. Detention of Asylum Seekers*, p. 59-61. See also *Rusu v. INS*, 296 F.3d 316, 323 (4th Cir 2002) and Frank M. Walsh and Edward M. Walsh, *Effective Processing or Assembly-Line Justice? The Use of Teleconferencing in Asylum Removal Hearings*, 22 Geo. Immgr. L.J. 259, 271 (2008).

[229] IACHR Report, ¶ 403.

[230] DHS/ICE, "Statement of Objectives."

[231] See generally American Bar Association, "Criminal Justice Standards on Treatment of Prisoners," (approved by the ABA House of Delegates in February 2010), available at http://www.americanbar.org/publications/criminal_justice_section_archive/crimjust_standards_treatmentprisoners.html.

[232] Supra, note 153.

[233] Christine Tartaro, "Watered Down: Partial Implementation of the New Generation Jail Philosophy," *Prison Journal,* vol. 86, no. 3 (September 2006), p. 286.

[234] A.E. Bottoms, "Interpersonal Violence and Social Order in Prison," in *Crime and Justice: A Review of Research*, vol. 26, eds. M. Tonry & J. Petersilia (1999), p. 243, n. 32. ("Additionally, within the direct-supervision approach, emphasis is placed on giving prisoners as much *autonomy* and *choice* as possible, consistently with the maintenance of a safe environment.")

[235] DHS/ICE, "Statement of Objectives."

[236] For asylum seekers and refugees, detention can amount to a penalty when, for example, asylum seekers are deprived of liberty for the mere reason of illegal entry or when detention fails the necessity test under Article 31(2) of the Refugee Convention. See Edwards, *Back to Basics*, p. 11, n. 64; see Noll, 'Article 31(Refugees lawfully in the country of refuge),' p. 1243, ¶ 96; see also IACHR Report, p. 86, ¶ 246 (U.S. immigration detention facilities visited by the Commission "employed disproportionally restrictive penal and punitive measures."); *Bell v. Wolfish*, 441 U.S. 520, 535 (1979) (a restriction or condition that is not reasonably related to a legitimate goal is punishment; pre-trial criminal detainees in state custody are protected from conditions that constitute punishment); *Youngberg v. Romeo*, 457 U.S. 307, 321-22 (1982) ("Persons who have been involuntarily committed are entitled to more considerate treatment and conditions of confinement than criminals whose conditions of confinement are designed to punish").

[237] 2009 DHS/ICE Report, p. 2.

[238] W. Raymond Nelson, "The Origins of the Podular Direct Supervision Concept: An Eyewitness Account," *American Jail*, vol. 2, no. 1 (1988), p. 10. See also Atlas, "Changes in Prison Facilities," ("The primary assumption of operation [behind the direct supervision model] was that a normalized environment would evoke normal behavior.")

[239] Tartaro, "Watered Down," p. 291. See also Bottoms, "Interpersonal Violence," p. 205. ("Enhanced physical restrictions can often reduce levels of violence due to restrictions on opportunity but may also sometimes lead to a loss of legitimacy that can escalate violence.")

[240] Human Rights First interview with Steve J. Martin, April 1, 2011. Also, Jeanne Woodford (former warden, San Quentin State Prison, former Acting Secretary of the California Department of Corrections and Rehabilitation) told Human Rights First, "The more you give people in custody, the better behaved they are, because they have more to lose... The degree of freedom of movement granted to inmates should be as much as possible, based on behavior.... Idleness is a terrible problem." (March 22, 2011) William Collins (former director of the American Correctional Association's Correctional Law Project, former head of Corrections Division of Washington State Attorney General's Office, editor of *Correctional Law Reporter*) suggested, "In a civil detention facility, detainees would presumptively be given a lot of responsibility over their interactions with each other. This would be premised on a philosophical shift." (March 16, 2011). Michele Deitch (criminal justice and juvenile justice policy expert, University of Texas Law School and LBJ School of Public Affairs) suggested that civil immigration detention might replicate conditions of trustee camps, which permit a high degree of freedom of movement, but place them inside a secure perimeter. She noted, "A secure perimeter is for public safety purposes. Perimeter security should be distinguished from conditions inside a facility... Criminal history of detainees should not affect the conditions inside the facility; it could be a risk factor, but far more determinative of custody classification would be the person's institutional behavior." (April 15, 2011)

[241] Robert Worth, "A Model Prison," *The Atlantic Monthly*, November 1995, available at http://www.theatlantic.com/past/docs/issues/95nov/prisons/prisons.htm; and Todd R. Clear, George F. Cole, and Michael D. Reisig, *American Corrections* (Independence: Wadsworth Publishing, 2005), p. 352-53.

242 Id.

243 Physicians for Human Rights, *Punishment Before Justice: Indefinite Detention in the U.S.* (Washington, DC: Physicians for Human Rights, 2011), p. 14, available at https://s3.amazonaws.com/PHR_Reports/indefinite-detention-june2011.pdf.

244 2009 DHS/ICE Report, p. 21.

245 Human Rights First interview with Jeanne Woodford, March 22, 2011.

246 Human Rights First interview with Steve J. Martin, April 1, 2011.

247 Human Rights First correspondence with Martin Horn, March 22, 2011.

248 Human Rights First interview with Berks County staff member, November 23, 2010.

249 Tim Irwin, "In rural Pennsylvania, a model of civil immigration detention," *UNHCR News*, January 6, 2011, available at http://www.unhcr.org/4d25c4fb6.html.

250 Because BTC holds more men than women, the facility has arranged access to outdoor recreation and the law library such that male detainees receive a much greater level of freedom of movement than the women. This inequity results from the layout of the facility and the population numbers, but it is not acceptable; facility designs should not be approved if they do not provide equal conditions for male and female detainees. The ABA 2010 Criminal Justice Standards on Treatment of Prisoners provide that "[l]iving conditions for a correctional agency's female prisoners should be essentially equal to those of the agency's male prisoners, as should security and programming." Standard 23-3.2. Human Rights First's other concerns at the time of our tour in September 2010: detainees wear prison jumpsuits; physician did not speak Spanish, despite overwhelmingly Spanish-speaking detainee population; no psychiatrist, dentist, or pharmacist on staff; facility lacked cafeteria as well as confidential attorney-client meeting space (since rectified); severely out-of-date law library, including a complete absence of materials necessary to prepare an asylum applications; absence of list of free and low-cost legal service providers next to telephones in the women's dorms, in violation of detention standards; and all hearings were conducted via videoconference, despite the existence of a fully functioning courtroom and judge's chambers in the facility.

251 "Fact Sheet: T. Don Hutto Residential Center," Immigration and Customs Enforcement, http://www.ice.gov/news/library/factsheets/facilities-hutto.htm (last modified March 24, 2010).

252 The lawsuit was brought against ICE by the American Civil Liberties Union, the ACLU of Texas, the University of Texas School of Law Immigration Clinic, and the international law firm of LeBoeuf, Lamb, Greene & MacRae LLP on behalf of 26 immigrant children detained with their parents at Hutto. For complete information about the lawsuits and the settlement, see "ACLU Challenges Prison-Like Conditions at Hutto Detention Center," ACLU, March, 6, 2007, available at http://www.aclu.org/immigrants-rights-racial-justice/aclu-challenges-prison-conditions-hutto-detention-center.

253 Human Rights First interviews with assistant field office director and Hutto medical staff, December 8, 2010.

254 Human Rights First tour of ICA-Farmville, September 24, 2010.

255 For more information, see the U.S. Federal Bureau of Prisons web site at www.bop.gov.

256 Human Rights First calculations based on federal Bureau of Prisons daily facility population data available at http://www.bop.gov/locations/weekly_report.jsp. Includes daily population of FPCs, FCIs, and low-security satellite camps as of 9/19/11.

257 ICE/DRO Detention Standard: Classification System, Part V(C).

258 ICE/DRO Residential Standard: Personal Hygiene, Part V(1.).

259 2009 DHS/ICE Report, p. 19.

260 Human Rights First tour of ICA-Farmville, September 24, 2010.

261 Karnes County IGSA.

262 Telephone conversation with senior ICE official, September 14, 2011.

263 Physicians for Human Rights and Bellevue/NYU Program for Survivors of Torture, *From Persecution to Prison*, p. 191.

264 2002 UN Special Rapporteur Report, ¶ 54.

265 UNHCR, *Mission to the United States of America*, ¶ 28.

266 IACHR Report, ¶ 436(i).

267 U.N. Econ. & Soc. Council (ECOSOC), *Standard Minimum Rules for the Treatment of Prisoners*, adopted by the First United Nations Congress on the Prevention of Crime and Treatment of Offenders, held at Geneva in 1955, and approved by the Economic and Social Council by its resolution 663 C (XXIV) of July 31, 1957 and 2076 (LXII) of May 13, 1977, ¶ 88(1) (hereinafter cited as Standard Minimum Rules for the Treatment of Prisoners). International standards also confirm that unconvicted persons should be treated in ways, and detained only in conditions, that are appropriate to their unconvicted status. Principle 8 of the Body of Principles provides that "[p]ersons in detention shall be subject to treatment appropriate to their unconvicted status." UN Body of Principles, principle 8. The United Nations Standard Minimum Rules for the Treatment of Prisoners and the American Convention on Human Rights also require states distinguish between the convicted and unconvicted, and detain the unconvicted only in conditions appropriate to their status. See Standard Minimum Rules for the Treatment of Prisoners, ¶ 84-5 (referencing "untried prisoners" who "are presumed to be innocent and shall be treated as such."); Organization of American States, *American Convention on Human Rights, "Pact of San Jose", Costa Rica*, 22 November 1969, art.

5(4), available at http://www.unhcr.org/refworld/docid/3ae6b36510.html (hereinafter cited as American Convention on Human Rights). ("Accused persons shall, save in exceptional circumstances, be segregated from convicted persons, and shall be subject to separate treatment appropriate to their status as unconvicted persons.") The Body of Principles provides that unconvicted persons "shall, whenever possible, be kept separate from imprisoned persons." UN Body of Principles, principle 8.

[268] Human Rights First, *U.S. Detention of Asylum Seekers*, p. 18.

[269] This is the practice at Douglas County Corrections (127 detainees), Baker County Sheriff Department (250 detainees), Etowah County jail (349 detainees), Ramsey County Adult Detention Center (66 detainees), McHenry County Correctional Facility (315 detainees), Sherburne County jail (115 detainees), Freeborn County jail (75 detainees), and Jack Harwell Detention Facility (100). Human Rights First interviews with local service providers, August 2010, March 2011, and September 2011, http://www.bakerso.com/corrections/inmate-info, and http://www.cecintl.com/facilities_sf_tx_017.html. It is also the practice at Pinal County Jail (Arizona), which holds more than 400 detainees daily. At Pinal County, detainees are restricted to using video to meet not only with visiting family and friends, but also with their attorneys. ACLU of Arizona, *In Their Own Words*.

[270] 2009 DHS/ICE Report, p. 24.

[271] For example, at Mira Loma Detention Center in California, which holds 1,190 detainees, family visiting hours are limited to Saturdays and Sundays from 7am to 3pm. At LaSalle Detention Facility in Louisiana, which holds 998 detainees and is located 230 miles from New Orleans and 140 miles from Baton Rouge, families may visit on Saturdays, Sundays, and holidays, from 8am to 4pm. They are limited to just 30 minutes. Neither facility permits contact visits.

[272] See ICE, *2008 Operations Manual*, Part V, 32(5)(B), and INS, *2000 Detention Operations Manual*, "Visitation," Part III(A).

[273] In March, April, and September 2011, Human Rights First conducted an informal survey among Detention Watch Network members, who work with detained immigrants across the country, and visited 17 facilities in person in the course of our research. We have learned that the following facilities do regularly permit contact visits: T. Don Hutto Residential Center, Elizabeth Detention Center, Hudson County Jail, Monmouth County Jail (with advance permission), Berks Family Residential Center, ICA-Farmville, Port Isabel Detention Center (on special request), Eloy Federal Detention Facility (though visitation space is insufficient for the volume of legal and non-legal visits), Karnes County Correctional Center, and Broward Transitional Center.

[274] 2009 DHS/ICE Report, p. 24.

[275] "Visiting periods should be of adequate length. Visits with counsel and clergy should not be counted as visiting time, and ordinarily should be unlimited in frequency. Pretrial detainees should be allowed visiting opportunities beyond those afforded convicted prisoners, subject only to reasonable institutional restrictions and physical plant constraints. For prisoners whose confinement extends more than [30 days], correctional authorities should allow contact visits between prisoners and their visitors, especially minor children, absent an individualized determination that a contact visit between a particular prisoner and a particular visitor poses a danger to a criminal investigation or trial, institutional security, or the safety of any person." ABA, "Criminal Justice Standards," Standard 23-8.5.

[276] "Physical contact shall be permitted between every prisoner and all of his or her visitors throughout the visiting period, including holding hands, holding young children, and kissing." Section 1-09 (f). The standard provides that before and after a visit, prisoners "may be searched solely to ensure that they possess no contraband." 40 Rules of City of New York, § 1-09(g)(1).

[277] See 9 N.Y. Comp. Codes R. & Regs. § 7008.6 ("(a) Physical contact shall be permitted between a prisoner and his visitors"); see also 9 N.Y. Comp. Codes R. & Regs. § 7008.2 ("(b) The visiting area shall be designed so as to allow physical contact between prisoners and their visitors."). The standard provides that before and after a visit, prisoners, "prior and subsequent to each visit, may be searched solely to ensure that they possess no contraband." 9 N.Y. Comp. Codes R. & Regs. § 7008.7.

[278] As of August 31, 2011; detailed research on file with Human Rights First.

[279] Federal Bureau of Prisons Program Statement 5267.08, "Visiting Regulations," § 18 ("PROCEDURES §540.51. h. (2) Staff shall permit limited physical contact, such as handshaking, embracing, and kissing, between an inmate and a visitor, unless there is clear and convincing evidence that such contact would jeopardize the safety or security of the institution. Where contact visiting is provided, handshaking, embracing, and kissing are ordinarily permitted within the bounds of good taste and only at the beginning and at the end of the visit.")

[280] For example, Woodford told Human Rights First, "Contact visits are important to the mental health of inmates."

[281] Commission on Safety and Abuse in America's Prisons, *Confronting Confinement*, p. 36.

[282] At ICA-Farmville (Virginia), for example, a facility for detainees with no criminal history, metal toilets are spaced about two feet apart in a long row, without dividers, and separated from the sleeping areas by just a low wall. Theo Lacy and El Centro Service Processing Center (both in California) also deny privacy in toilet and shower areas to detainees.

[283] Human Rights First interview with Steve J. Martin, April 1, 2011.

[284] Human Rights First correspondence with Martin Horn, March 22, 2011.

[285] Human Rights First correspondence with William C. Collins, March 16, 2011.

[286] Human Rights First tour of Essex County Jail, February 24, 2011. Other ICE-authorized facilities visited by Human Rights First that provide toilet and shower privacy for detainees include Berks Family Detention Center (curtains around toilets), T. Don Hutto Residential Center (curtains around toilets),

South Texas Detention Complex (shoulder-height dividers between toilets and showers), and Port Isabel Detention Center (as of December 2010, toilet dividers were being installed in housing areas holding low-risk detainees, according to the assistant field office director).

287 ABA, "Criminal Justice Standards," Standard 23-3.1.

288 At Essex County Jail, there are interior "courtyards" in each dormitory area for level 2 detainees (considered medium risk), visible to everyone and accessible all day, which have openings in the roof to the sky and contained a couple of rusty old exercise machines. On the day that Human Rights First toured the facility, no one was using the "outdoor" recreation area, likely because of an unbearable stench coming from the nearby sewage treatment belonging to the Passaic Valley Sewerage Commission. (See supra note xx for details regarding environmental concerns around Essex County jail.) At the Northwest Detention Center, the only recreation available to detainees was an indoor gym with open windows and a roof. At Glades County Detention Center, in south Florida—one of the hottest and sunniest climates in the country—the outdoor recreation lacks shade. See Human Rights First, "U.S. Detention of Asylum Seekers," p. 21, which describes similar situations at Elizabeth Detention Center, San Diego Detention Center, and Pearsall Detention Center, among others.

289 ICE, *2008 Operations Manual*, "Recreation," Part V(A), and INS, *2000 Detention Operations Manual*, "Recreation," Part III(A) and (B).

290 2009 DHS/ICE Report, p. 21, 22.

291 IACHR Report, ¶ 323.

292 Mark D. Martin and Paul Katsampes, *Sheriff's Guide to Effective Jail Operations* (Washington, DC: National Institute of Corrections, U.S. Department of Justice, 2007), p. 46.

293 Worth, "A Model Prison."

294 Human Rights First tour of Port Isabel Detention Center, December 6, 2010.

295 Human Rights First interview with Steve J. Martin, April 1, 2011.

296 ABA, "Criminal Justice Standards," Standard 23-3.6.

297 While Krome's outdoor recreation area itself is a good model, detainees' access to the outdoors is limited to just one hour per day.

298 Female detainees at BTC can access the outdoor space for just four hours a day, unlike the male detainees. This significant disparity should be addressed so that the women's access is increased. The ABA 2010 Criminal Justice Standards on Treatment of Prisoners provide that "[l]iving conditions for a correctional agency's female prisoners should be essentially equal to those of the agency's male prisoners, as should security and programming." Standard 23-3.2. Human Rights First was also concerned that the exercise machines in the outdoor space were old and rusty.

299 Martin and Katsampes, *Sheriff's Guide*, p. 41.

300 Commission on Safety and Abuse in America's Prisons, *Confronting Confinement*, p. 12. Steve J. Martin, former general counsel of the Texas Department of Corrections, told Human Rights First that "there is nothing better than programming" to create a safe environment for detainees (April 1, 2011).

301 In its 2010 report, the Inter-American Commission on Human Rights noted that "ICE's history when it comes to providing free, low-cost telephone service to immigrant detainees has been deplorable." IACHR Report, ¶ 309. It cites ongoing problems with connectivity for both free and paid calls, sound quality, and cost. In January 2010, the DHS Office of the Inspector General raised concerns about ICE's lack of oversight of the financial aspects of its telephone service contracts, making it easy for detainees to be overcharged for calls. (DHS—Office of Inspector General, *Immigration and Customs Enforcement Management Controls over Detainee Telephone Services* (Washington, DC: DHS, 2010), OIG-10-36, p. 6, available at http://www.dhs.gov/xoig/assets/mgmtrpts/OIG_10-36_Jan10.pdf. In 2008, the DHS OIG identified problems with existing telephone services including lack of incentive for the contractor to improve performance, significant connectivity issues, and lack of oversight of rates and contractor profits. (DHS—Office of Inspector General, *Review of Immigration and Customs Enforcement Detainee Telephone Services Contract* (Washington, DC: DHS, 2008), OIG-08-54, p. 3-4, available at http://www.dhs.gov/xoig/assets/mgmtrpts/OIG_08-54_May08.pdf. In 2007, the Government Accountability Office found "systematic problems" with the system that allows free calls to consulates, pro bono legal service providers, nongovernmental organizations, and the DHS Office of the Inspector General, and noted that "ICE's lack of awareness and insufficient internal controls appear to have perpetuated telephone system problems for several years." (Government Accountability Office, *Telephone Access Problems Were Pervasive at Detention Facilities; Other Deficiencies Did Not Show a Pattern of Noncompliance* (Washington, DC: GAO, 2007), GAO-07-875, p. 10, available at http://www.gao.gov/new.items/d07875.pdf.

302 Emails sent via TRULINCS are subject to monitoring, even those emails between an inmate and his attorney—unlike USPS-delivered correspondence between an inmate and his attorney. For more information about TRULINCS, see "TRULINCS FAQ," Bureau of Prisons, last modified October 4, 2011, accessed October 4, 2011, http://www.bop.gov/inmate_programs/trulincs_faq.jsp. The costs of the system are covered by commissary and phone charges, plus a charge of 5 cents per minute for the service itself.

303 Human Rights First interview with ICE assistant field office director, December 8, 2010. He said that he would permit male detainees the same access (Hutto houses women only).

304 Human Rights First interview with Steve J. Martin, April 1, 2011.

305 Edwards, *Back to Basics*, p. iii.

306 See box, p. 27.

[307] As described in the body of this report, a standardized risk assessment is one of many necessary steps that can assist in allowing for significant cost-savings by shifting some individuals from detention to Alternatives to Detention or release on bond. If the data used during risk assessment is linked appropriately to a centralized database through this tool, the new tool may provide much-needed information about release processes and classification decisions at all facilities in the detention system, improving oversight and accountability. ICE still needs to develop triggers for re-running the assessment, so that, for example, asylum seekers who have passed their credible fear screening interviews and are thus no longer subject to mandatory detention will automatically be re-assessed for release. The agency also needs to set aside sufficient resources to evaluate the tool through a validation process after it has been fully implemented, to ensure that it is leading to appropriate individual outcomes, and to revise scoring or other aspects of the tool if it is not.

[308] See box, p. 27.

[309]. See box, p. 27.

[310] Specifically, Congress should amend § 235 and 236 of the Immigration and Nationality Act to allow all detention decisions to be made on an individual basis.

[311] 2009 DHS/ICE Report, p. 18.

[312] ABA, "Criminal Justice Standards," Standard 23-8.1 ("Governmental authorities should strive to locate correctional facilities near the population centers from which the bulk of their prisoners are drawn, and in communities where there are resources to supplement treatment programs for prisoners and to provide staff for security, programming, and treatment"); Standard 23-8.5 ("To the extent practicable, a prisoner should be assigned to a facility located within a reasonable distance of the prisoner's family or usual residence"; Standard 23-9.4 ("Correctional authorities should facilitate prisoners' access to counsel").

[313] Supra, note 18.

[314] The Commission was created by Congress in the Prison Rape Elimination Act (PREA) of 2003 to propose standards to "prevent, detect, respond to and monitor sexual abuse of incarcerated or detained individuals throughout the United States." In its final report, in June 2009, the Commission found that "[a] large and growing number of detained immigrants are at risk of sexual abuse. Their heightened vulnerability and unusual circumstances require special interventions." *National Prison Rape Elimination Commission Report*, Ch. 9. The Commission developed supplemental standards to apply to any facility holding ICE detainees, but these standards have yet to be adopted by the Department of Homeland Security. Instead, DHS incorporated less detailed sexual abuse standards into the draft 2010 PBNDS. Earlier this year, the Department of Justice proposed standards under PREA that exclude from coverage facilities holding primarily immigrant detainees.

[315] Tartaro, "Watered Down," p. 291-92.

[316] See e.g., James B. Jacobs and Elana Olitsky, *Leadership & Correctional Reform*, 24 Pace L. Rev. 477 (2004).

www.ingramcontent.com/pod-product-compliance
Lightning Source LLC
Chambersburg PA
CBHW051420200326
41520CB00023B/7310